Growing Camellias

Growing Camellias

Neil Treseder
and
Edward Hyams

NELSON

THOMAS NELSON AND SONS LIMITED
36 Park Street London W1Y 4DE
PO Box 18123 Nairobi Kenya

Thomas Nelson (Australia) Ltd
19–39 Jeffcott Street West Melbourne 3003

Thomas Nelson and Sons (Canada) Ltd
81 Curlew Drive Don Mills Ontario

Thomas Nelson (Nigeria) Ltd
PO Box 336 Apapa Lagos

First published in Great Britain, 1975

Copyright © Neil Treseder and Edward Hyams, 1975

ISBN 0 17 143024 7

Printed in Great Britain by
A. Wheaton & Co., Exeter

Contents

Plates

Introduction

The popularity of the camellia is now such that it vies with the rhododendron as the most popular evergreen shrub. Whilst camellias cannot tolerate the intense cold which the hardier rhododendrons can endure, they have more attractive foliage than most of their competitors, their flowers usually last longer and mostly open over a longer period, sometimes for several months. They make excellent wall plants.

Camellias provide distinctive cut material for indoor decoration, either as specimen blooms or as cut sprays. They have a considerable vase life when kept in a cool environment, and their glossy foliage shows up well in artificial light.

Camellias are also very rewarding as greenhouse plants, as has been demonstrated by the fine collections at the Royal Gardens at Windsor, by Sir Giles and Lady Loder at Leonardslee, and elsewhere.

Because they will tolerate drier soil conditions and prolonged exposure to hot sunshine they make excellent tub plants for terraces and patios. They are, of course, even more at home in sunless situations and will flourish in woodland shade.

Their versatile nature, coupled with the varied colours, forms and season of their flowers, makes them adaptable for gardens in all but the colder areas. Although basically intolerant of alkaline soils, they are not so fastidious as rhododendrons, and will tolerate fairly alkaline conditions if supplied with ample reserves of humus and planted in maximum shade.

The authors acknowledge as sources of much useful information *A Revision of the Genus Camellia* by J. Robert Sealy (1958) and contributions of various authorities to past editions of the *American Camellia Year Book* and the *International Camellia Journal*; also *Camellia Nomenclature* published by the Southern California Camellia Society, which provides the most extensive listing of named cultivars of Camellia available.

Readers interested in joining the American Camellia Society should write to the Secretary at Massee Lane Camellia Gardens, Box 212, Fort Valley, Georgia 31030. The International Camellia Society's secretary is Mr. Charles Puddle, Bodnant Gardens, Tal-y-Cafn, Colwyn Bay, Denbighshire, U.K.

PART 1

by
Edward Hyams

I

Camellias in the Wild

The genus *Camellia* belongs to the family *Theaceae*, and the only member of the genus we shall not deal with in this work is the most important, economically, of them all, the Tea plant, though it has a certain inconspicuous charm when in flower and is hardy enough to be grown in the south-west of Britain. The genus consists of between sixty and seventy species, and it is confined to China, Japan and India. The general character of the plants, which are all either trees or shrubs, is too familiar to need description, but for the record we should say that the leaves are always evergreen, alternate—that is, not opposite each other in pairs—and more or less toothed on the margins. The flowers of most species are large, showy, borne in the leaf axils, usually solitary, but sometimes in pairs or, rarely, threes. The fruit is a woody capsule carrying only a few seeds.

We are concerned in this book not to write a botanical treatise, of course, but to write about the nature and cultivation of camellias as garden plants which everyone can grow. As only a minority of the species are important in this context, we shall say something about these and ignore the others. We take the ones which matter to us here in alphabetical order, and readers who do not think it necessary to know anything about the wild nature of the plants they are going to grow or are growing can skip this chapter entirely. But it is sometimes a good idea to understand one's garden plants thoroughly if one is to grow them well, and such understanding is enhanced if one knows a little about them as wild plants.

13

CAMELLIA CUSPIDATA

This is an evergreen bush of erect habit but slender growth which seldom exceeds a height of 6 feet. It is a native of China and was introduced to Britain by the great plant collector Wilson, who was working for the famous nursery firm of Veitch about 1912. Its leaves are shaped like lance-heads and are between 1½ to 3½ inches long but rarely as much as an inch wide. They are shining dark green on the upper face, paler on the underside. The flowers, carried on short stalks in the leaf axils, are pure white and about 1½ inches across. It is one of the parents of *C.* x 'Cornish Snow'.

CAMELLIA JAPONICA

This is by far the most important species from the gardener's point of view, whether for its own sake or as the parent of some good hybrids. Again an evergreen, it is a shrub as commonly met with, but it can be a tree to 30 feet or more. Some of the old *C. japonica* trees in Cornish gardens are probably that tall, and in Portugal and the Southern States of the U.S.A. we have seen them up to 40 feet. The deep and lustrous green leaves are oval and up to 4 inches long, usually tapering to a short point, hard and leathery in texture. The flowers of the wild species are red and are between 2 and 4 inches in diameter with five to eight petals and conspicuous golden stamens.

Geographical forms of Camellia japonica

In Japan there are three distinct types which appear to have adapted themselves in the wild to variations in climate and environment. These have now been classified by Japanese botanists thus:

(1). The Snow Camellia (*C. japonica* subspecies *rusticana*) = *C. rusticana* Honda.

(2). The Apple or Yakushima Camellia (*C. japonica* var. *macrocarpa*) = *C. hayaoi*.

(3). The Bush Camellia (*C. japonica* var. *spontanea*).

The distinguishing features of these three types are briefly as follows:

(1) The Snow Camellia (*C. japonica* subspecies *rusticana*) = *Camellia rusticana* Honda.

This is the most distinct of the three and was claimed to be a separate species by Honda, the Japanese botanist, in 1937. It is native to the most northerly limits of camellia distribution in Japan, occurring from altitudes of over 4,000 feet down to the coast of the Sea of Japan. This is an area of heavy snowfall and the plants remain covered under several feet of snow for several months each winter. In the wild, Snow Camellias have a distinctive growth habit, their flexible trunks or branches tending to trail along the ground where they often become buried in decaying vegetation. They show a pronounced tendency to throw up sucker growths from their roots and buried trunks. In summer they are shaded by deciduous trees among which they grow. Their glossy leaves have three distinguishing features: the leaf stalks or petioles are short and bear microscopic hairs on their undersides as are found in *C. reticulata* and *C. saluenensis*. There appears to be a relationship between the density of petiolar hair and a plant's ability to withstand the effects of heavy winter snow. The leaf venation is conspicuously translucent, showing complex reticulation, and the leaf margins have denticulate (finely and sharply toothed) serrations whereas the marginal pattern of most other camellia leaves is crenate (having rounded teeth).

Snow Camellias are very variable in flower form and colour and they apparently hybridize naturally with *C. japonica*, where both species intermingle. Their petals are

15

narrower, spread horizontally and bilobed at the apex. Their stigmas are split longitudinally into three.

It remains to be proved whether they will tolerate colder conditions in cultivation than other camellias when not protected by deep snow. It is reported that they do not flourish without adequate snow cover in the wild. It is now believed that the wide range in flower form and colour of camellia cultivars is inherited largely from the Snow Camellia.

Well-known cultivars bearing traces of petiolar hairs include 'Arejishi', which also shows the characteristic leaf-serration of the Snow Camellia, and 'Otome', which has few traces of petiolar hair but has the characteristic translucent venation.

(2) The Apple Camellia (*C. japonica* var. *macrocarpa*)
= *C. hayaoi*

Natural distribution begins in the southernmost part of Kyushu (the South Island of Japan) spreading extensively further south on the island of Yakushima. It is also found on other islands northward to Okinawa.

The Apple Camellia resembles the Bush Camellia in growth with leaves inclined to be narrower. The flowers are small with the appearance of never opening fully. These have characteristic hairs at the base of their styles. The fruits are large and spherical. It is not likely to interest camellia breeders and is probably less hardy than (1) and (3).

(3) The Bush Camellia (*C. japonica* var. *spontanea*).

This has the widest distribution, extending from the south-west of Kyushu along the coast, and northwards following the sea-shore off the main island of Honshu. It has not been found on Hokkaido (the North Island of Japan) but it also grows on the islands of Chusan at the mouth of the Yangtzu River in China, as well as on Formosa, the Ryukyu Islands and in southern Korea. It is there a plant of maritime environments, tolerating full exposure to sun and wind. Bush Camellias flourish in parts of Japan where the summers are too hot for the larger-leaved rhododendrons.

The flowers and foliage of wild Bush Camellias are reported to be remarkably uniform in appearance. Most have red flowers with five petals, rarely six or seven, and no double forms have been discovered. This fact seems to indicate that the many Japanese garden cultivars which have originated over centuries are selections from natural hybrids between Bush and Snow Camellias. During scrub clearance, to make way for agriculture and forestry operations, many unusual forms were transferred to farmyards and cottage gardens, where they have been preserved to provide interesting material for future investigation.

In his *Revision of the Genus Camellia* (1958) Sealy classifies *C. japonica* var. *spontanea* as a synonym of *C. japonica* var. *macrocarpa*.

Although the cultivars which come under the heading *C. japonica* were long treated primarily as greenhouse shrubs they are perfectly hardy, withstanding over 30 degrees of frost, indeed below-zero temperatures, without taking any harm. They are the oldest camellias in cultivation in the West, for they became known to European gardeners early in the eighteenth century. Native, as we have seen, to the mountains of Japan, Korea and Eastern China, those which were first imported into Britain were probably specimens of the varieties long cultivated by Chinese gardeners, for it was from China that we had our first camellias. Most *C. japonica* cultivars flower in the open from April to June, though some begin to blossom in mid-winter. *Camellia japonica* is readily distinguishable from its allies because of its hairless gynoecia and the presence of cork-warts on the under-surfaces of its leaves.

CAMELLIA MALIFLORA

It seems not to be known for sure where this one came from, but it is thought to be Chinese. Apparently it has not been seen in the wild by any professional botanist and it was introduced, as a cultivated plant, in 1818 by Captain Rawes. It is a very bushy evergreen shrub to about 8 feet with broadly lancehead-shaped leaves up to 2 inches long and more than half as wide. Its double, flesh-pink flowers are about 1½ inches across. They open from January to March under glass but here it will only blossom out of doors where grown against a sunny wall. In America it is grown under the cultivar name of 'Betty McCaskill'.

CAMELLIA OLEIFERA

The true species is rarely seen in cultivation. It is a low, spreading shrub, but it can grow tall when trained against a wall or if planted in a very sheltered situation. The stiff, leathery, saw-edged leaves are 3 to 4 inches long and lack the lustre usually associated with camellias. The flowers, single white, are 1 inch in diameter, and begin to open in November. It somewhat resembles, and is frequently confused with, *Camellia sasanqua* 'Narumigata', which masquerades in many nurseries as *C. oleifera*.

CAMELLIA PITARDII

This is a variable Chinese species intermediate between *C. reticulata* and *C. saluenensis,* forming a tall open-branched bush with thin, lax, well-spaced leaves 2½–4 inches long, dark green and glabrous, their margins being markedly denticulate. The flowers have five or six petals, the colour ranging from rose to white. According to the geneticist Dr E. K. Janaki Ammal, both *C. pitardii* and *C. reticulata* are hexaploid ($2n = 90$), whereas *C. saluenensis* is diploid ($2n = 30$).

CAMELLIA RETICULATA

The history of this camellia is curious. Long before it

was known to Western botanists in the wild, it was introduced to Britain, in 1820, as a cultivated plant of which the wild ancestors had never been seen by Western eyes. It had, in fact, been cultivated by the Chinese for many centuries and was much planted in their temple closes. This cultivated form is a tall and vigorous small tree, bearing semi-double rose-pink flowers which are 6 inches in diameter. It can be seen in a number of English gardens usually growing against a wall.

George Forrest, the great plant collector, who was working in West China and Tibet in the course of four major expeditions between 1904 and 1932, sent home seeds of a number of wild camellias. One of these, collected in 1932, the year of Forrest's death from heart failure in a remote Chinese province and listed under his number 25352, turned out to be the wild form of this camellia, native of Yunnan at altitudes up to 9,000 feet. It is fairly hardy in Britain but it flowers so early that the flowers are sometimes ruined by frost.

It is a tree, or a big shrub, and may reach 30 feet or more, with leathery, elliptical leaves up to 4 inches by 2 inches, dark green, rather dull than glossy. Its 3-inch flowers vary from rose-pink to blush pink and open in March, or even in February. In Southern China it attains a height of 50 feet in open pine forests at altitudes of 6,000 to 9,000 feet.

CAMELLIA SALUENENSIS

The Salween River Camellia is one of the parents of the important race of hybrids called *Camellia x williamsii* which we shall come to presently. It is a very bushy and luxuriant evergreen shrub to as much as 15 feet with pointed leaves averaging about 2 inches by 1 inch, dark, glossy green, and not as leathery in texture as *C. japonica*. Its rather funnel-shaped flowers, about 2 inches or less across the open mouth, vary from white to carmine and are produced singly or in pairs in the leaf axils, very early in the spring. It comes from Yunnan and it was discovered there by Forrest in 1924 and introduced under his number 17686. It is not as hardy as *C. japonica,* but is nevertheless hardy enough for most British gardens.

CAMELLIA SASANQUA

This was first brought to England as a cultivated plant in 1811 by the master of an East Indiaman. (So, for that matter, were some of the earliest introduced *C. japonica* plants.) As a wild plant it is native to the southern islands of Japan, Kyushu, Shikoku and others. It is a hardy evergreen shrub with shining dark green leaves between $1\frac{1}{2}$ and 3 inches long and 2-inch flowers, white in the type, but with pink variants which have enabled the Japanese, and much later Western, plant breeders to obtain a range of colours. It flowers from November to February.

CAMELLIA TALIENSIS

An evergreen shrub to 8 or 9 feet, or a shrubby tree to 20, this is another of George Forrest's introductions from Yunnan. Its cup-shaped white flowers are from 2 to $2\frac{1}{2}$ inches in diameter, usually opening about midwinter. It is not as hardy as the species mentioned earlier, and should be given wall protection except in the most favoured gardens.

These are the principal species of value and interest to gardeners, but some others also come into the picture, or at least they are beginning to do so, not so much for their own sakes as for their qualities as parents of future hybrid camellias. Among these the Taiwan species, *C. brevistyla,* and *C. caudata,* and three of four others are attracting the

attention of plant breeders; the Indo-Chinese species, notably
C. amplexicaulis, which has purple flowers, are tender, of
course, but, crossed with *C. japonica,* they could yield cultivars with a new range of colours. One of them, *C. flava,*
has yellow flowers and could, therefore, be of very great
value in this respect, unless its tenderness is linked with its
colour.

Camellia tsaii, with long, tapering, twisted leaves and
copious small white flowers is in cultivation and has even
received a Royal Horticultural Society Award of Merit.
There are still others. But the important ones are those
which we have described.

II

Soils and Situations

In nature, camellias are plants of the woodland and mountain soils. Such soils are open, spongey or gritty, rich in organic material, both the coarse, raw material, the carrion of vegetation, and the end product of the decay of that material, humus. The roots of the camellia are fine, fibrous and densely crowded; they are neither adapted to nor is there any need for them to grow far from the plant and deep into the subsoil. For, like rhododendrons, camellias rely upon the fact that in their natural conditions the fertility of the soil is being constantly renewed from above, by forest leaf-fall and waterborne nutrients. Thus, camellias are among those plants which form a root-ball, a dense and stable mass of top-soil held together by the system of fibrous roots; this makes it easy to transplant them at almost any age, but it also makes it very necessary to see that they are planted in the kind of soil they can manage. For example, they will not even begin to grow in dense clay, the kind of soil that roses, flowering prunus of all kinds, or the flowering crabs, can exploit. Camellias really thrive in a light to medium lime-free loam enriched with leaf-mould and peat above good drainage.

In most ordinary gardens the drainage is not bad, but where it is poor, something must be done about it. In some parts of Britain there is, beneath the subsoil, a layer of impervious clay, and that can mean that water is held above it, thus waterlogging the subsoil. It may be necessary to

22

break through it and fill in the holes with drainage material, gravel for example, or broken crocks, but never mortar-rubble or limestone chippings. Such drainage material should be packed very tightly, making sure that the water thus drained away can subsequently escape, and it may be necessary to put in some land-draining half-pipes. On the whole these special measures are not necessary, especially where the fall in the level of the water-table caused by our enormous and wasteful consumption of water has been so great.

There is a natural device which keeps soil in perfect water-balance from the camellias' point of view: deep-rooted trees, such as oaks, which draw water from a considerable depth to transpire it from their leaves, whilst reducing evaporation from the top-soil by shading it. On the other hand shallow-rooted trees, such as cypress and yews, take water out of the top-toil itself and may keep it so dry that nothing can grow in it.

Before describing the preparations it should be said that camellias are calcifuge plants, that is, they will not grow in chalk soil, or in soils rich in soluble limestones of any kind. In this respect they are not as fussy as are most rhododendrons or, for example, kalmias, but their distaste for lime has to be taken into account. They grow best in neutral and acid soils rather than soils whose pH—the symbol used by chemists to express acid–alkaline balance—is above 7. Simple soil-testing outfits are now available at most garden shops which will quickly reveal the pH of your soil.

There is more to be said about this, however. The first thing is that, excepting the case of a really chalky soil, it is not very difficult to lower the pH and acidify the soil sufficiently to accommodate camellias. There are various ways: raking-in dressings of ordinary commercial sulphur will do it; or you can make your garden compost with heavy dressings of sulphate of ammonia on the heap, which will produce an acid compost; or, where the pH is already 7 or only a

23

small fraction higher, the trick can be done by forking in a very liberal amount of acid peat, the black sedge peat sold as 'Rhododendron' peat.

The other point worth noting is this: the debility, which may amount to chlorosis and in time to death, of calcifuge plants in limy soils is not caused by any positive action of lime on the plants. Lime is not poisonous to any plant; on the contrary, all plants without exception need *some* calcium. But plants vary in their ability to take up salts of iron from the soil; calcifuge plants are plants which are relatively bad at doing this. Lime locks up these iron salts in a chemical combination which makes it impossible for camellias, rhododendrons, kalmias and the like, to get at them. You could perfectly well grow camellias, then, even in chalk, if you could find a way of getting iron into them. Well, such a way has been found. There are certain compounds of iron salts, known as chelates, in which the iron is so firmly held in combination with another element that the lime, the calcium, in the soil cannot get at it and combine with it; but this chelated iron, soluble in water, is readily available to the plants. The earliest chelates, while better than anything we had had before, were not very effective. But the latest, in commerce first as Sequestrene 138 Fe, and now more commonly met with as Murphy Sequestrene, is very effective indeed. Moreover it has been our experience that few plants respond so quickly, especially in youth, to dosing with this Sequestrene, as do camellias. A young plant, its leaves yellow from chlorosis, will often turn deep green and begin to grow well within three weeks of treatment. Does this mean that camellias can now be grown in soils high in lime? The answer would seem to be 'Yes', provided that the feeding with Sequestrene is regular, and strictly maintained. This will not necessarily lead gardeners on limestone soils and chalk to grow camellias, for many gardeners feel, and perhaps rightly feel, that what they cannot grow 'naturally' and without special measures, they would rather not grow at all.

To return now to the question of top-soil preparation. We are beginning with an ordinary garden loam. On the area to be planted with camellias spread half a barrow-load of 'rhododendron' peat per square yard, as much leafmould or well-rotted garden compost—up to half a barrow-load per square yard—as you can get; one barrow-load per 4 square yards of the coarsest silver sand; really old and thoroughly rotted farmyard manure if you can get it; and, per 4 square yards, one large handful of John Innes Base Fertilizer. If you have a rotary cultivator rotovate this time and again until the dressings are thoroughly mixed into the garden's natural loam. If not, then it will have to be done by forking and raking.

Now this preparation is a very thorough one and quite expensive. Is it essential? No. If the loam of your garden is light or medium, fertile, holds water well while being well drained, and has a pH below 7, then camellias will grow in it anyway. But camellias are long-lived trees; they will last longer than you will, and will, if well-grown, give you more delight from their lovely flowers and evergreen foliage than almost any kind of lesser garden plant. It is worth while, if you can do it, to prepare for them thoroughly and give them a really good start in your garden.

SITUATION

No camellia really likes to be fully exposed to either the sun or the wind. We have found the following things about camellias to be true: that perfectly hardy camellias which are quite unharmed by 20 or 30 degrees of frost in still conditions, are badly damaged and can, in youth, even be killed, by freezing east winds persisting for a week or more; that camellias grow faster in sheltered sites than where they are exposed to wind; that young camellias which were going back on a site in full sun, recovered and grew away well when moved into a shady position.

There can be no question that camellias are better in shady than in sunny situations. A plant can use sunlight only in proportion to the rate at which its leaves can absorb carbon dioxide from the air, since CO_2 is the raw material of photosynthesis for which process sunlight supplies the energy, and there is no point in having more energy than there is raw material for it to work on. The leaves of some plants absorb CO_2 and distribute it throughout the body of the leaves much more quickly than those of other kinds. The rate depends on the internal structure of the leaves. True, exposure of camellias to sunshine simply means that they will not make use of all the energy provided; from that point of view there will be no harm done. But exposure to full sun means faster transpiration of water and a need to take up more water through the roots: water loss may be faster than gain, and although the plant may not flag visibly, there will be a check to growth. Since, then, camellias can get all the light they can use in the broken shade of trees where transpiration will be slower, they are better off in shade than in sun.

What camellias really like, then, is (a) shelter, provided by, for example, a belt of conifers, or a fine dense hedge of holly, thorn or privet, or the shape of the land, or woodland trees. And (b) the broken shade of taller trees which will filter the sun's rays, and keep the plants cool and in partial shade at least during the heat of the day.

It is quite possible that your garden cannot provide these conditions. In that case, make the camellia planting the occasion for planting, at the same time, those shelter shrubs and shade-casting small trees which will create the right conditions.

In town gardens there is, of course, another solution. Most

town gardens are already pretty well sheltered from the worst of the winds by buildings. The right side of the house for your camellias, in a town garden, is the north; camellias are very good north-wall plants, provided the soil, apt to be full of builder's rubble, at the foot of the wall has been taken out and replaced with the kind of mixture we have described.

IRRIGATION

We have repeatedly found that very slow growth of young camellias, and even total check to growth, has been caused by shortage of water. It may seem inconsistent with our insistence on very good drainage for these plants, but it is not. Good soil drainage swiftly removes all *surplus* water from the soil; it does not, if the soil texture is good, remove soil-water properly so called. What, then, does the expression 'soil-water' mean? Soil of good texture, any soil in really good condition, consists of agglomerations of particles of mineral and organic substances held together by the resins which are an element of humus. There is probably an electro-chemical effect at work here, but we need not go into that. Each such tiny ball of material has a skin of water and in that water plant nutrient salts are held in solution, so that the feeding roots of plants can take them in. Now if you put a number of spheres, marbles for example, or green peas, into a box, they do not fit together tightly, excluding all air spaces; owing to their shape there are interstices between them. In the case of soil these spaces should be filled with air. If they are filled, other than temporarily, with water, then that soil is waterlogged and any plants standing in it for a prolonged period, with the few exceptions of the genera which prefer those conditions, will die from root suffocation. This is the surplus water which drainage is designed to remove; it should not and will not remove the

27

true soil-water, the water held by each soil particle as a skin.

But if there is not a pretty constant *flow* of water through the soil, then what happens? The roots of the plants take up the soil water, it is not replaced, the soil becomes dust, and the plants first flag and ultimately die. So, then, what we need is a constant movement of water through the soil, without surplus water remaining long in the soil. Soil engineers recognize a soil condition which is the optimum for plants of all kinds. It is called 'field capacity', and it is that state when, following a period of drainage after rainfall (or irrigation), the soil is holding, by capillary attraction all the water it can against the force of gravity. This is the condition which the gardener cultivating camellias should aim at maintaining during the period of active growth, but it must also be said that all plants (other than aquatics) seem to prefer considerable variations in soil moisture. Nurserymen still recall the remarkable growth made by most plants during an abnormally dry summer about ten years ago when the heathland of Dartmoor became covered with cracks into which one could insert one's hand.

Evergreen plants with the rich and copious foliage of camellias transpire an enormous amount of water from their leaves. Either, then, you must make sure, in rainless spells, that they are supplied with it at the roots at least as fast as they get rid of it by transpiration and evaporation from the soil surface; or you must check transpiration by raising the humidity of the surrounding atmosphere. Better still, you can do both, which is why we believe that the best means of irrigating camellias is by one of those rainers or sprinklers which throw a fine fountain of water high, wetting first the leaves and then the soil. Cheap plastic hose, and the range of irrigating devices, has now made it easy for any gardener to build up an irrigation system without calling in a plumber; it is very simple to provide, in advance, a water-point to which, in dry spells, a length of flexible sprinkler-

Plate 1. 'EXBURY TRUMPET'. An early and remarkably weatherproof cultivar of *C. saluenensis*, with single funnel-shaped flowers

Plate 2. The wild form *C. reticulata* from Yunnan introduced by George Forrest in 1924

Plate 3. *C. reticulata* 'CAPTAIN RAWES'. The first variety of *C. reticulata* to be introduced into Western gardens (1820)

Plate 4. *C. reticulata* 'ROBERT FORTUNE'. Another cultivar of early introduction which was subsequently lost sight of for over a century

hose can be attached to give the camellias an artificial rain for a few hours when they need it.

It is well worth while to do this for no plants respond so gratifyingly to water in plenty. In their native lands of China and Japan and the high mountains of northern India, Camellias receive far more rain than they receive naturally in Britain, excepting in a few special places—Dartmoor, the Welsh mountains, parts of Scotland—where the rainfall is much higher than the average for the country.

III

Buying and Planting

Camellias are stocked by nurserymen in two, and sometimes three, age-groups. First as young plants in pots; these will have a small trunk and a few branches, as a rule, and will be between a foot and 2 feet tall. As camellias flower young they may already be flowering. Secondly, older plants growing in the open nursery beds, more substantial than the ones in pots, and between 2 and 4 feet tall, yet still young in their general appearance, the growth already woody, but rather thin. Thirdly, it is possible to buy, at certain nurseries, mature bushes, with stout trunks well branched; they are, of course, quite dear, for they have taken perhaps ten years of space, and of care, to grow; and there are certain difficulties involved in transplanting them. Still, it can be done by those in a hurry and with the money to indulge their impatience. Neil Treseder deals with this subject in a later chapter.

The process of producing these shrubs will have been something as follows. Camellias are raised by nurserymen from cuttings which are rooted under mist—the now universal mist-propagation method has more or less replaced the old closed-case method, although that can still be used. Once the cuttings are well rooted on the mist-bench, they are planted into very small pots and returned to mist conditions for weaning prior to transfer to a cool greenhouse for growing on. Twelve months later when about a foot high, they are re-potted into slightly larger pots in which they are grown on for a further twelve months, which brings them to saleable size of 15 to 18 inches, usually with several branches. Some nurserymen then transfer them to open-air plunge beds to harden them off prior to sale.

Conscientious nurserymen who really understand camellias never sell pot plants straight out of the greenhouse unless they do so at the customer's request and on the understanding that the customer knows he is getting a 'soft' plant. As camellias grow much faster in a cool-house than when planted or stood out of doors, the temptation to grow them on as fast as possible and and get a good price for fine, large plants is very great. But such plants are likely to succumb to severe frost unless they are carefully hardened off by the purchaser before being planted out. Unfortunately, the kind of nursery which sells such unhardened plants is unlikely to admit it, so the customer may be getting a poor bargain without knowing it.

So if you buy the smaller and therefore cheaper plant in a pot, it is unlikely to have been hardened off in the open air. Remember that no pot- or container-grown plant can be termed 'pot-established' until its roots trace their way around the inner surface of the container. The uninitiated may consider such a plant to be pot-bound, a condition about which much ridiculous nonsense has been written in the past. How often have we noticed that the healthiest and strongest camellia in a batch is one which was accidentally repotted into a size smaller pot than its companions. It is far better to have a well-nourished plant in a small pot than one which has been over-potted into a container many sizes larger than necessary for its immediate needs. Such over-liberal treatment may even prove fatal, for it seems that container-grown plants do not flourish until their root tips have reached the walls of their prison.

If you decide to buy larger plants, those which have had one or two seasons of growth in the open ground of the

31

nursery (and such plants will cost you more, of course) , you will do one of two things. Order the plants out of the nurseryman's catalogue, having decided, from the plates and descriptions in this book, what you want; in that case the nursery will deliver them to you in the planting season, say November; or you may go to the nursery or garden centre, preferably by appointment, choose your plants, and bring them away with you in your car. Open-ground plants will be lifted with the soil-ball intact, wrapped in coarse sacking or perhaps in polythene, with a strong tie round the base of the trunk, to preserve it while it is being transported.

PLANTING

If the soil has been prepared in the manner we suggest in Chapter 2, you will need no special material for planting the camellias. If it has not, then it will be as well to have by you a supply of granulated peat. If you buy one of the dried and packed brands, such as Irish Moss Peat, it is absolutely essential to get this thoroughly impregnated with water before you use it. Peat is peculiar stuff; once wet it will hold an incredible amount of water for a long time; but if buried dry it acts like a sponge and it can cause the death of your plants by depriving them of moisture. So open the bale or pack a week before you want to use it, spread it out and make a ring with it, fill the space in the middle of the ring with water, and mix peat and water in the same way that a builder's labourer mixes cement. This must be done thoroughly unless you have bought the kind of peat which is not dried before sale; but in that case do not forget, when making price comparisons, that you are buying a lot of water.

If you are planting small plants from pots, soak in water for a few seconds if dry, dig a hole larger than the pot, knock the plant out of its pot without disturbing the root ball, and plant, filling in all round it with a mixture of the ordinary garden loam and peat to which has been added a handful of general fertilizer. Do not on any account let the level of the pot soil be lower than the level of the garden soil; on the contrary, let it be a little higher. The same thing applies to the larger plants with their soil ball wrapped in sacking. Remove the sacking, put the soil-ball into a hole much larger than itself but quite shallow so that the level of the top of the soil-ball is higher than the level of the ground all about it, and, again, fill in with a mixture of the loam you took out when digging the hole and moist peat enriched with several handfuls of garden fertilizer.

If you have grown other kinds of flowering shrubs, especially the deciduous kinds, roses for example; or if you have planted fruit-trees in your time, and if, before doing so, you either read a handbook or took advice, you will have been told that woody plants must be planted very firmly, that you cannot overdo this, and that it is a good thing, after planting, to ram the soil all round the newly planted tree or shrub with a baulk of timber, or stamp it hard with your heel. All this is quite true but does *not* apply to the very delicately fibrous-rooted, flowering evergreens like camellias and rhododendrons. Certainly the soil must be made firm all round the newly planted camellia; but only with pressure of hands and arms. Camellias do not grow happily in densely impacted soil; so the soil round them should be made firm, but *not* rammed down.

If, as we have suggested, you have planted your new camellias shallowly, with the top of the pot-soil or the soil-ball slightly higher than the level of the surrounding soil, there is now one more thing to be done. If the ground is at all dry, water the plant in, not too heavily; and then spread round it a mulch of mixed peat and leaf-mould and even old and very well-rotted farmyard manure, or of pure peat, and do it so that this mulch makes up the difference between the two levels. As we explain below, nothing better promotes the quick and healthy growth of shrubs as a good mulch of suitable material, and it was with mulching in mind that we suggested shallow planting. For repeated mulching can easily bury a camellia or rhododendron too deeply for its own good, unless it is foreseen and provided for in this manner.

What, now, about staking? If the site chosen for the camellias is protected from high winds, as we have suggested that it ought to be, it should not be necessary to stake such small plants as we have had in mind. If it has been necessary to compromise, choosing a site which is usually protected from wind but not from all directions, so that the plants may occasionally be exposed, then taller ones should be staked for the first two years to prevent them from rocking. Actually, camellia branches on young plants are so flexible that little disturbance is conveyed to the roots by wind movement.

When we come to the case of the larger plants, the transplanting into your garden of really large bushes of camellias, perhaps 6 feet tall and with a heavy top, the case is different. It is true that the root-ball will be very heavy and will thus anchor the plant, but rocking is still likely if there should be a gale, as there invariably is just when you do not want it.

To replant a big camellia bush, first dig a hole about twice as large as the root-ball and very slightly shallower than the root-ball measures from base to soil-surface. You will next want two oak stakes about 3 feet long, 3 inches thick, and well pointed at one end. Drive these into the ground exactly opposite each other at the extreme periphery of the hole until there is at least 18 inches under ground and only 18 inches left above ground. Now plant your camellia, standing the soil-ball centrally in the hole, and filling in with the spoil from the hole mixed with moist peat, using a great deal of peat. Firm the soil and water thoroughly.

Cut a long strip of sacking about 6 inches wide and bandage

with it the trunk of your camellia bush, or the stoutest trunk if there are several, not too tightly, at the same height as the tops of the two stakes. Next, nail two 1-inch thick and 3-inch wide battens of wood, to join the two stakes, one on each side of the trunk of the camellia at the point where it is bandaged. Finally, cross-bind the trunk and battens with really strong cord, keeping the cord well within the area of the trunk protected by the bandage of sacking.

This will hold the bush steady even in a very high wind, and enable its roots to take a hold of the ground. It is a less unsightly device than bracing, but it must not be left in place for too long. It should be frequently inspected, and it should be removed after, at most, two years.

The principal difficulty in establishing really large plants like this, after transplantation, is this: the constant loss of moisture by transpiration through the leaves will, for at least a year, tend to be at a greater rate than the plant, not yet properly re-rooted into the ground, can replace by its root-action. That results in loss of turgidity, flagging of the leaves, leaf-fall, and possibly death. So the gardener's job is to prevent this happening. You will, of course, mulch the plant after watering, in the manner already described for the smaller plants. And much can be done by frequent irrigation, of the kind which wets the leaves and not merely the soil, especially during dry spells. There is another and more sophisticated way of dealing with this problem: you can buy from good garden shops, though you may have to order it, a substance known as S.600 Plastic Transplanting Spray, which, mixed in the way described by the makers for your benefit, can be sprayed onto the foliage of the camellia bush, preferably before transplanting, using the apparatus you normally use for pest- and fungus-control spraying. This sets into a transparent but impermeable film all over the leaves—it has, of course, to be applied very thoroughly—and seals their surface off from the air for a suitable length of

35

time. You have, by this treatment, temporarily suspended all transpiration, and therefore all loss of water, by the plant. By the time that this artificial skin wears off, the roots of the camellia should have taken a new hold and should be working again.

We have successfully moved very large evergreens, including camellias, without recourse to this method. But it is true that they received daily attention in the matter of watering both soil and foliage, and keeping the mulch renewed.

Prior to transplanting very large specimens we advocate the complete removal of all weak and spent branches by cutting them out flush with the trunk with a sharp knife or secateurs. If you carefully check each branch it is surprising how many only have leafy shoots at their extreme ends, all minor growths having been gradually swamped by stronger branches. Remove all of these before you commence to lift your veteran camellia. By so doing you may well reduce the foliage by one third, transforming it maybe from a dense bush to one with well-spaced branches. But you may also preserve its life for a further half-century or more.

We have safely transplanted camellias of up to eighty years of age, sometimes using more drastic measures than these, and please do harden your heart and remove all the flower buds. Any which are allowed to mature after such shock treatment are unlikely to be very good. After transplanting, the critical period comes in April and May, when the weather may suddenly change from cool and wet to a prolonged period of hot sun and drying winds. Then temporary screening or shading will be most beneficial, the best type being one which sifts the wind and allows dappled light to reach the plant. Laths nailed their own width apart to a supporting framework will provide an ideal protection from both sun and wind.

If, in spite of careful treatment, a recently transplanted

specimen shows signs of acute distress and the leaves begin to dry out, then more drastic measures may be advisable. Severely prune the worst affected branches so that all leafy growths are removed, even to the point of reducing the plant to a framework of shortened, leafless branches. These should be kept cool and moist either by regular irrigations and shading, or by covering with polythene sheaths in which some vent holes should be made, or by binding with a complete sheathing of damp moss. Whatever method is used it must be retained until the new growths are an inch or two in length. These will probably be very numerous and overcrowded, and judicious thinning may be necessary the following spring.

IV

Manuring and Feeding

This subject is dealt with separately in the chapter which deals with growing camellias in pots for the greenhouse and house. Here we are concerned solely with camellias in garden borders and shrubberies.

It is not usually necessary to use chemical fertilizers on camellia plantations. If, when you have your soil analysis before planting, you find that there is a serious deficiency of one of the major nutrient elements, then you can bring it up to the desirable level by using an artificial manure. Soil analyses do not, in the ordinary way, tell you anything about the trace elements necessary to plant health. But trace-element deficiencies do not kill plants until long after they have been revealed by symptoms which enable one to diagnose the particular deficiency and make it good. We have something to say about that below, but it should be emphasized that trace-element deficiencies are comparatively rare.

They will, in any case, be made good automatically if a policy of annual mulching is carried out; and this mulching will also provide all the feeding that the plant needs provided the mulch be of the right kind. Ideally, it should be a compost made more or less as follows, but we realize that one component, farmyard manure, will probably be impossible for most gardeners to obtain.

If dead leaves, grass-mowings, bracken if you can get it, soft hedge clippings, and the small, very young weeds collected during hand-weeding, are composted in an open pen made of wire netting nailed to four stakes, with layers of farmyard manure, they will provide the mulch which camellias will thrive on. You begin in November, and you end in November, so that each lot of compost takes just a year to make. You can turn it once or twice if you like, but it is not really necessary. Nor does it matter if the compost is not absolutely rotted down, the process will be completed after it has been spread under the camellia bushes. By doing that spreading in November you clear the composting pen for the next year's supply.

If you cannot get farmyard or stable manure, you can use, to activate and enrich your compost, an occasional all-over sprinkling of an ordinary balanced fertilizer. You can mix the compost with peat to make it bulkier, before you use it. But it should be remembered that while peat is very valuable indeed in improving the texture of soil, giving it just the structure which plants thrive in, it is doubtful whether it has much value as a source of plant nutrients.

This policy of bulk manuring by mulching is the best. If, for whatever reason, it is more convenient for you to use plant food materials which have little bulk, then stick to the slow-acting organic ones, such as bone-meal, fish-manure and dried hops, or one of the manures derived from seaweed. You should use small quantities, probably not more than two handfuls per bush per year, and apply the stuff just after flower-fall, when the bush can do with a tonic; repeat when flower-bud initiation begins in July or August.

I.C.I. have produced an excellent organic-base garden fertilizer which is obtainable at most garden shops under the trade name of 'Garden Plus'. It is sold in a range of sizes from packets to 50-kilo sacks. We have used it on a very wide range of garden plants with excellent results, both as a pre-planting application, thoroughly dug into and mixed with the soil to a depth of 9 to 12 inches or more, and also as top dressings before and during the periods of active growth.

We have used it extensively for camellias with excellent results and we have even found it beneficial to rhododendrons and azaleas, a practice which would doubtless horrify many experienced growers of such plants.

Never dig in an application of fertilizer around an established bush. Either leave it on the surface to wash in or lightly rake or hoe it into the top inch or so of soil. Better still, mix it with an organic mulch, being sure to cover the surface beneath the outer branches where the feeding roots are situated.

The policy of making your mulch also the source of plant food, and of using compost made with healthy plant and animal material, will keep the soil at the camellia roots provided not only with the salts of nitrogen, potash and phosphorus which are the three principal nutrients, but also with trace-qualities of all the other elements which are required, although only in minute amounts. As we have said, if one or more of the necessary elements is missing, the plant will show symptoms and you can do something about it.

Chlorosis, manifest as an all-over paling and finally as a yellowing of the leaves, is most commonly caused by calcium-induced iron deficiency; if that symptom appears, therefore, your first move should be to assume that that is the trouble and give the plant a dose of Sequestrene 138 Fe. It should respond in three weeks or less; you can get a quicker response by spraying a very weak dose of the Sequestrene onto the leaves, wetting both sides. If, within three weeks, the leaves have assumed, or are visibly assuming, their normal deep green colour, then you know that your diagnosis was correct and that you need do nothing more but watch that plant for any sign of the trouble recurring, which it should not do for a year at least. If the plant does not respond and remains an unhealthy yellow colour, then you can be fairly sure that the chlorosis has some other cause. For, unfortunately, there is more than one cause of chlorosis in camellias. A sulphur deficiency causes much the same symptoms as an iron deficiency. But it is extremely rare in Britain, rather less rare in America; and it is easily corrected by raking a few handfuls of flowers of sulphur into the soil.

If the chlorotic colour is not pale yellow, but a deeper, orange-yellow, then the most likely cause is a deficiency of magnesium. This, again, is cheap and easy to supply: a weak solution of ordinary Epsom salts, sprayed onto the leaves, will give quick results; and a long-term cure can be attended to at the same time by raking Epsom salts into the soil so that rainwater will carry it, in solution, into the roots. The same kind of chlorosis, however, can be caused by deficiencies of manganese or boron. Suitable salts of both elements can be bought at good garden shops, in small sachets, and applied to the soil in solution. White patches or areas fading to dead white on the leaves are probably a symptom of copper deficiency, and can be dealt with in the same way.

It should be said again, and emphatically, that such troubles are uncommon and probably often correct themselves, in time, without any special steps being taken, as the mulching programme begins to take effect. Nine hundred and ninety-nine times out of a thousand chlorosis in camellias is caused by too much lime in the soil, and this is something we have, if our suggestions about soil preparation have been followed, avoided in advance.

41

V

Propagation

(1) BY CUTTINGS

From both the commercial and amateur points of view the most important way of propagating camellias is by cuttings. The amateur can, of course, get camellia cuttings to root without any apparatus at all; but with fairly cheap mist-propagation outfits on the market, suitable for the small, amateur propagation bench, and with close propagating cases fitted with electrical bottom heat thermostatically controlled even cheaper, most gardeners who do any propagating at all will have one or the other. We shall therefore assume that the reader has either one of the propagating cases now on the market, or an amateur's mist bench, or that he has the handiness to make a suitable case for his small number of cuttings without any help from us. Actually, a deep wooden box with a sheet of glass over it will do at a pinch.

The less sophisticated amateur, who yearns to root a few camellia cuttings but has no such aids as a mist unit or bottom-heated frame, need not close this book with an air of envy or disappointment. He or she can, in fact, root camellia cuttings with no more costly equipment than a large sweet jar, obtainable at almost any sweet or confectioner's shop. The screw cap must cover an opening large enough to enable one to insert one's hand into the jar.

The procedure is extremely simple. Procure some moss

(preferably of the sphagnum type usually found around moorland bogs and pools) and chop it up or shred it with a sharp scissors. If no moss is available some peat moss will suffice. Wet it thoroughly and then squeeze out all surplus moisture before mixing with one third of its bulk of coarse sand, adding a few lumps of wood charcoal if available.

Fill one third of the sweet jar with this mixture, then prepare and insert the cuttings as later described (page 45). Screw the lid down tightly and place in a north-facing window. Unscrew the lid for only a very brief period for the removal of any dead or decaying leaves or cuttings. Excessive curiosity may prove fatal, as some of the humidity trapped in the jar escapes each time it is opened.

Rooting takes place more rapidly in a sunny window but the jar must first be shaded on the outside by painting with white emulsion paint or sticking a coating of white paper around it to diffuse the light and prevent scorching. A small inspection panel may be kept unmasked on the side of the jar facing into the room. As a rule no watering is necessary since the original moisture is trapped in the jar.

After rooting, transfer the cuttings into the smallest pots available, potting gently and not too firmly, watering and returning to the sealed jar for seven to ten days before gradually weaning by removing the lid for longer periods each successive day and spraying with water on each occasion. An old scent spray is ideal for this purpose.

The man who has invested in a mist-propagating outfit will be an advanced enough gardener to need no help from us in the management of his apparatus. We can concentrate on the larger number of readers who will be using some kind of closed frame. But in both cases the compost to be used will be identical, and that is the next matter to consider.

We have used the word 'compost' but in fact the material which fills the bottom of a propagating case, over the heating wires, is not really a compost at all. It is a medium to stick the cuttings into mechanically satisfactory and holding water, but without nutrients. There are a number of such mediums; you can use pure peat; or pure silver sand; or vermiculite or some other substance such as perlite or a mixture of two or more of them.

We make the following suggestion. If you are able, perhaps because you have retired or have private means or for whatever reason, to give daily attention to your propagating case, then the medium in which to strike camellia cuttings should be pure, coarse silver sand, which you buy at any good garden shop, and nothing else. If you are not able to do this, by reason of your gainful occupation as the tax office calls it, then use a mixture of half coarse silver sand, half granulated peat, by volume—not weight, of course. The reason for the difference is this: the pure sand medium carries less risk of rotting the cuttings at the base and of fungus troubles, but it demands daily and copious watering. The sand-and-peat mixture, holding water tenaciously, does not demand daily watering, but carries a slight risk of rot or fungus troubles.

Right; you have your case ready, and the medium in place. When? From about mid-July, presuming you will be taking the camellia cuttings from bushes in the open. The kind of material you want will be ready between about mid-July and mid-September. One cannot get nearer than that.

Nothing is more difficult to convey in words, or easier to show in action, than the meaning of the words, so often used in gardening manuals, 'firm, half-ripened wood', which is the kind you should take for camellia cuttings. The cutting should consist of a short length of stem with two good buds on it in the leaf axils, more if you like, the stem being dark green but not yet woody, on the other hand not still soft and sappy either. Put the cuttings into a polythene bag as you take them and twist the end of it and knot it to close it. Loss of turgidity, however slight, is almost always fatal, and even partially wilted cuttings are useless.

Plate 5. *C. reticulata* 'LIONHEAD'. A Kunming *reticulata* cultivar, the large peony-form flowers have irregular, crinkled and arching petals

Plate 6. 'VILLE DE NANTES'. This striped and frilled semi-double sport of *C. japonica* 'Donckelarii' is often blotched with white

Plate 7. C. x 'LEONARD MESSEL'. An outstanding and free-flowering semi-double hybrid of *C. reticulata simplex* and *C. x williamsii* 'Mary Christian', raised at Nymans, Sussex

There are three things you can do at this stage if you like, but we have had quite good results without them. The first is to cut a slanting face on the base of the cutting, using a very sharp knife, thereby exposing a greater surface of the kind capable of making root. Secondly, you can cut off half of each of the two or three leaves left on your cutting to reduce the area of transpiration. But this also reduces the area of photosynthesis and in our opinion this is a practice of very little, if any, value. Thirdly, you can dip the base of your cuttings into a root-inducing hormone. Whether you do these three things or not, you now plant the cuttings up to the base of the lower leaf into the compost in the case, and replace the cover. Cuttings should be about 4 inches apart in rows about 6 inches apart.

Where propagating material is scarce it is possible to raise plants from leaf-cuttings, but this takes a year longer, for the orthodox stem cuttings involves the rooting of a shoot which has already had one growing season to develop. Leaf cuttings are best made from much riper growth than stem cuttings, say from October to January, and consist of a leaf with a small section of the shoot to support it and with the embryo growth-bud in the axil. There are two types of leaf cutting: one consists of the leaf and bud attached only to a small 'shield' or scoop out of the stem; the other is the so-called 'mallet' type, made by making a transverse cut immediately above and below the leaf stalk. They need careful handling, shallow planting, and they often fail to produce any shoot growth for twelve months after rooting. Still, in the end they will grow and make good plants.

The propagating case thermostat should be set at between 65°F and 70°F, the case should be aired and watered daily and the cover of the case shaded with plastic gauze. There is nothing more to be done, now, but these things until the cuttings are rooted, except the removal of decaying material.

It is rather difficult to say how long this will be. About as close an estimate as we can give is this: the quickest cuttings

45

will root in three weeks, the slowest in three months. It is almost entirely a matter of the condition of the material taken as cuttings. Caught at exactly the right moment, cuttings of camellia root quite quickly; if the material is too soft it may not root at all and if too hard it will take longer.

Growth from the buds on the cutting and the production of new leaves does not prove that the cuttings have rooted. In a good, warm, close case with a humid atmosphere and enough light, cuttings often grow by drawing on the nourishment stored in the stem, without roots. But a gentle tug at the cutting will reveal either some resistance or none, and resistance means that roots have grown and are holding onto the sand or compost. Do not immediately remove the cuttings from the propagating case. Another week's growth will ensure an adequate root system. They can then be taken out of the case and replanted in $2\frac{1}{2}$-inch pots. This time, of course, the compost should not be sterile, but nourishing; it should also be either neutral or on the acid side of neutral. We have had excellent results with John Innes No. 2 compost with the sand content omitted, for camellias appear to prefer a fairly heavy medium in which to grow.

When the rooted cuttings have been planted into their pots they should either be returned to the propagating case for a week or two and given frequent airings; or, if left out on the greenhouse bench, then carefully shaded and syringed twice daily, until they are hardened to the less favourable conditions. As they harden and begin to grow, these weaning treatments can be discontinued. Careful weaning is even more important in the case of camellia cuttings rooted under mist. Ideally, the mist-propagation unit will include a weaning attachment. In any case, newly rooted cuttings should not be removed too brusquely from either the close atmosphere of a case or the humidity of a mist bench. There must be an interval of gentle treatment.

As we point out when describing camellia propagation in commercial nurseries, there is no point in, and much to be said against, potting on young camellias into larger pots until their roots have quite filled the smaller pots. The young plants will do better as they are and need not be moved into larger pots for at least a year. Although young camellia plants will have to be hardened off by plunging them out in the open, in their pots, for a considerable time before they are moved out permanently, they should not be put out of the greenhouse immediately. Here is a rough timetable: it has been found at Treseder's Nurseries that the two most successful starting months are September and February.

Cuttings taken and planted in propagation case:	15 Sept. 1971
Cuttings rooted:	30 Oct. 1971
Cuttings planted in 3-inch pots and returned to propagation case:	7 Nov. 1971
Removed to greenhouse bench:	21 Nov. 1971
Transferred into 5-inch pots about:	1 Nov. 1972
Grown on in greenhouse till	June 1973

So hardening off begins in June/July 1973. The object of keeping young plants under glass for so long is simple: camellias grow faster under glass and one might as well have a relatively large and densely rooted young plant to put out, as a small and fragile one.

Hardening off begins by plunging the young plants outside the greenhouse, by covering the pots with granulated peat and shading them from sunlight at first. If you put them out in May instead of June they should be protected from late frosts. As nights get warmer they can be left without protection to benefit from the evening dews. By late summer or early autumn they should be ready for planting out, although the careful gardener may prefer to overwinter them in a frame which can be covered in very severe weather, to plant out in the following May.

Camellia cuttings tend to flower, and even flower freely,

when quite small. As camellia seedlings do not do this, the reason would seem to be that a piece of camellia wood taken as a cutting is, in one sense, as mature as the parent plant. At all events, flowering checks the growth of the young plant and flower buds should be removed as fast as they appear during the first two years of the young plant's life.

(2) BY GRAFTING

Grafting entails the uniting of a young shoot, known as a scion, from a selected variety onto a well-rooted understock. This method of propagation becomes necessary with varieties which are difficult or impossible to root from cuttings, as are the double *Reticulatas*. It is also an advantage where propagating material is limited, as is often the case with new varieties. By grafting onto mature understocks much of their vigour can be diverted into the scions so that faster growth results than where younger understocks are used.

Nurserymen prefer to graft onto pot-established understocks because these can be readily transferred, firstly to a controlled environment, such as a greenhouse or frame, to promote the early growth initiation desirable for spring grafting. Secondly, they are moved to the propagator's bench or other convenient place for the actual operation of heading back and grafting. Thirdly, the grafted plant or plants can then be transferred to a close propagating frame or pit where it is best to lay the pot or pots on their sides, the scion being uppermost where side grafting has been resorted to, so that the union benefits most from the upward trend of sap flow. From a nurseryman's point of view, understocks established in quite small pots, 2½-3 inches in diameter, are preferred because they are easy to handle and occupy less space than larger ones.

The grafting of camellias may be carried out at most times of the year but the normal periods are early spring, whilst the scions are still dormant, and late summer, when the young growth has almost ripened. If the growth buds on the scions have already started into growth it may be advisable to remove them, since their continued development may exhaust them before union can take place. Such material would only be used where no better opportunity was likely to present itself.

Cleft grafting has been found the most successful method for propagating the cultivars and hybrids of *Camellia reticulata*. The best results are obtained by using young, vigorous, cutting-rooted understocks of *C. japonica* of such varieties as 'Contessa Lavinia Maggi', 'Conspicua', 'Monstruoso Rubra' and 'Optima', which have thick young shoots approximately corresponding in diameter with those of the scions of the mother plant.

August is usually considered the best month in British nurseries but the operation may be performed a month earlier where both stock plants and scions are grown under glass, or carried out at almost any time up to bud-break in spring. The growth should be at least half-ripe.

An ideal cutting instrument is a razor blade in a suitable holder. The terminal bud is removed from the understock and the stem sliced down the centre for 1 to 1½ inches. If the top of the stock has not yet commenced to ripen, first shorten it back into riper growth preferably making the transverse severance immediately above a leaf where there is a maximum cambial activity to heal over the cut surfaces and promote a union between stock and scion.

Next select a young shoot as scion from the parent plant on which the terminal bud has formed and the leaves have attained their normal size and texture. If the season's growth has not reached this stage it is advisable to delay operations for a while. Remove the lower leaves from the scion, leaving the top three or four, then cut downwards on opposite sides of the base to form an even, wedge-shaped point, an inch or so long, to match the depth of the vertical cut in the tip of the stock plant.

Before inserting the scion, neatly trim off the wafer-thin extreme tip of the wedge by placing it on a clean piece of wood and carefully cutting it transversely with a razor blade to remove any torn material or tissue so thin that it is liable to damage when the wedge of the scion is pressed firmly into the cleft in the tip of the understock. At least one side of stock and scion should coincide. In the event of uneven thickness causing protrusion on one side it is best to slice this away, provided such an operation does not penetrate deeper than the bark.

The two are now firmly, but not tightly bound together with Dutch cotton, grafting tape or raffia, making sure that the top of the wedge does not protrude above the tip of the cleft in the stock. If plastic grafting tape is used remember to remove it as soon as possible since it does not perish and will soon become embedded in the callus growth which follows.

The old habit of applying wax or similar covering to the union has been found unnecessary. Some propagators prefer to reduce transpiration by cutting away the end halves of the leaves on the scions, especially when dealing with larger leaved varieties. It is best not to remove any leaves or shoots from the base of the stock until the following spring since these help to ensure active root-growth.

Saddle grafting is a term applied to a reversal of the operation described above, the stock being cut to form the wedge and the scion slit upwards and opened up to fit over the tip of the stock like a saddle.

Side grafting operations are somewhat similar but the · stocks do not require heading back until after a successful union has taken place, and they need not be of similar diameter to the scions as is desirable with cleft grafting. The basal leaves are removed from the lower 3 to 4 inches of the stock together with any low branches. A shallow downward cut 1 to 1½ inches long is then made down one side of the cleared portion of the stem to open up a tongue-like section of bark, taking care not to extend deeply into the woody tissues.

The scion is prepared as described under cleft grafting; it is inserted firmly into the slit in the side of the stock, after carefully trimming across the point of the wedge, and is then bound firmly, making sure that at least one edge of the exposed cut surfaces coincides. Place grafted plants on their sides, scion uppermost, in a close, shaded frame and cover over their pots with damp sphagnum moss or peat moss to maintain a moist atmosphere. Sprinkle or spray with water regularly and commence gradual weaning after about six weeks by occasional ventilation and reduced shading.

A gentle bottom heat of 60°F to 70°F assists callus formation, the unions taking from three weeks to as many months according to temperature and time of year.

Grafting enables a nurseryman to supply an unexpected demand for a particular cultivar and to redeem kinds overpropagated or left unsold by using them as understocks. Quite large specimens can be grafted by enclosing them in polythene bags and more than one variety can be grafted onto the same understock if desired.

(3) BY LAYERING

Camellias can be propagated by layering. Two methods are practicable. If there is, on the bush to be propagated, a branch near enough to the ground to be drawn down so far that the smaller branches or twigs at the end of it lie on the soil, then there is no difficulty. A peg is driven into the soil below the branch, and the branch pulled gently down and firmly secured to it with rope or cord; or a rock may be laid on top of the branch where it is in contact with the

51

ground. The soil surface below the twiggy end of the branch must first be cleaned and some mixed peat and coarse silver sand raked in.

There will be, perhaps, half a dozen two-year-old twigs about a quarter of an inch thick at the end of the branch: all will make suitable layers. Leaving the three topmost leaves of each in place, strip those below them until you have 6 inches of bare twig. Half-way along this naked length, scrape away the bark at the lower side of the twig to expose an inch of naked wood. At the point where this touches the soil, drive a stout, short bamboo cane into the ground. Now bend the twig upwards in such a way that the inch of scraped wood can be buried 2 inches deep in the prepared soil, and the twig, now pointing upwards, can be tied, at two points, to the cane. Make the soil firm all round each layer. You can, if you 'believe in' them, dust the wound with a root-forming 'hormone' before you bury it.

We consider that March and April are the best months for this operation and that layers so made can be severed from the parent bush and planted into a frame for growing-on, one year later. (It would be safer to pot-establish them first.) Wood which has not rooted by then was probably more than two years old. It will root in time, but may take two or even three years to do so.

(4) AIR-LAYERING

The second method of layering can be used if it is impossible to pull any branch on the parent shrub near enough to the ground to make the terminal twigs lie on the ground, or where one wishes to root a portion of the top of a bush which may have sported and produced flowers of a different form or colour from the parent.

The twig to be rooted should not be more than two years old. Retaining at least three of its terminal leaves, remove those below for a distance of 6 inches or so, then notch or

wound the bark, or remove a ring half an inch wide mid-
way along the bare part of the twig. Take a small, stout
polythene bag and slit the bottom open: you then have a
polythene tube. Slip it over the end of the twig and bind it
firmly to the twig 3 inches below the wound in the bark.
You then have the twig in a sort of poke. Stuff the poke with
moist, chopped sphagnum moss, peat, or lime-free compost,
packing it tight. Then bind the top of the poke to the twig
as firmly as you did to the bottom.

The main difficulty with air-layering lies in keeping rain
from waterlogging the rooting medium and rotting the
young roots. These become visible through clear polythene,
or they may be easily felt as quite hard outgrowths by gently
squeezing the bag to check if fit for severance from the parent. A year after this operation you can cut the twig from
the parent bush just below the poke, cut away the polythene, and find the moss or peat or compost full of white
roots. The young camellia is then potted and carefully
weaned before being planted in the nursery frame as before.

(5) PROPAGATION BY SEED

There are probably only two occasions when the amateur
may wish to grow camellias from seed: if he is trying his
hand at hybridizing camellias; and if he happens to find
seed developed on one of his camellia bushes and feels that
it is a shame not to try to germinate the seed, 'just to see'.

Whether you buy seed or collect it from your own bushes,
it must be fresh. Like all seeds with a high content of oil,
camellia seeds, which are quite large, deteriorate and become
less viable with every day they are kept after ripening is
complete. The pod or shuck which carries the seed is a fruit
about the size of a crab apple. As soon as it cracks along its
divisions—late in October or early in November in the case
of *C. japonica*—the seed inside is ripe and can safely be taken
out and sown.

There are two ways of doing this: before germination, or after germination. The first is simple. Sow the seeds, which are as large as peas, 2 inches apart both ways in John Innes or Levington seed compost, covered half an inch deep, in seed pans, and put the seed pans into the propagating case at a temperature of 65° to 70°F. In gardens where mice are troublesome, protection will be needed, as mice are fond of camellia seeds. Germination should be within a fortnight but may take a month. The seedlings make a long tap-root before they make any fibrous root, so potting on should be as soon as possible.

The second method is not quite so simple but has the advantage of getting the young camellias onto their fibrous, feeding roots much sooner. The seeds are simply buried, as thick as you like, in pure silver sand and kept moist at about 70°F. After twelve days they are sorted out of the sand and those with no young tap-root replaced as before. Those which have a tap root are kept out. You have ready a pan of John Innes compost or sphagnum peat and the seeds are replanted in that, widely spaced, *after having half the root cut off* with a sharp pair of nail scissors, or a razor-blade. Unable to grow a tap root, the seedling produces fibrous root, which is what one wants it to do, of course. This sounds rather drastic but it works.

As soon as the seedlings are well established and growing, they can be potted on into 3-inch pots and thereafter treated as rooted cuttings. Most seed-raised camellias take many years before they commence to flower. Expert hybridizers reduce this period by artificial lighting to increase the day-length and sometimes by the use of such chemicals as gibberellic acid.

THE EFFECTS OF GIBBERELLIC ACID ON CAMELLIAS

What is gibberellin? It is best described as a complex

organic chemical compound which is a product of the growth process of the fungus *Gibberella fujikuroi*. Its formation is therefore similar to penicillin.

The first recorded use of gibberellin on camellias was by Lockhart and Bonner of the California Institute of Technology, who reported on their experiments in the 1957 edition of the *American Camellia Yearbook*. Gibberellins are produced naturally by growing plants, and they play an important role in regulating growth and responses to temperature and day length. Increases in growth of the parts of camellias treated with gibberellin indicate that they do not usually produce enough themselves to achieve their maximum possible growth rate. Artificial applications of gibberellic acid to camellias are therefore more a means of assisting nature than of diabolical interference with its natural processes.

Gibberellic acid affects camellias in several remarkable ways, and its use has recently become popular among camellia growers in America, so the craze is certain to spread to Britain before long. Gibberellin speeds the rate of seed germination and stimulates the growth of seedlings in the same manner as artificially prolonged day length. It also has a remarkable influence on earliness and flower size if buds are treated in late summer and autumn.

Seed treatment. Recent American experiments involving the soaking of camellia seeds in various concentrations of gibberellic acid showed promising results, the optimum concentration apparently being 100 parts per million for twenty-four hours.

Seedling treatment. Seedlings sprayed with a weak solution of gibberellic acid were stimulated into more vigorous and prolonged growth. The callus of recently grafted plants and the growth buds of scions have also responded to drops of the solution.

Flower bud treatment. Select well-developed flower buds in early autumn. Break off the adjacent growth bud and apply one drop of diluted gibberellic acid to the empty bud cup, using an eye dropper or hypodermic syringe. If very young or poorly developed buds are treated they will elongate and either drop off, fail to open or produce deformed flowers. Effectively treated buds commence to open abnormally early but take much longer to develop, and therefore present a greater weather hazard on outdoor bushes. The resulting flowers are often much larger and finer than those normally produced. Gibberellin sometimes delays petal abscission so that the outer petals die and wither whilst the inner ones are still fresh. The terminal portions of treated shoots are best pruned after treated flowers have developed or where response has been unsatisfactory, otherwise gibberellin may have a retarding effect on the subsequent season's growth from shoots which have been treated. It is best to treat only a few selected buds on any one plant. Successfully treated buds usually show a rapid increase in size within a few weeks of treatment and then remain static until they are about to open, whereupon a more gradual swelling starts when the whole process of flower development proceeds at a slower rate than normal. It causes some flower buds to develop and open much earlier so that an extended flower season becomes available, but this factor is irregular and unpredictable.

In some seasons and on some varieties the effect of 'gibbing' is disappointing and the treated buds produce flowers inferior to normal ones.

Gibberellic acid has to be applied in a highly concentrated solution, and it is not readily soluble in water, so the usual method is to add household ammonia or alcohol (the latter often causing damage to plant tissues) drop by drop until the tiny, suspended crystals have completely dissolved.

Messrs Plant Protection have now overcome this problem by producing, in tablet form, a gibberellic acid formulation under the trade name 'Berelex', which is readily soluble in cold water. 'Berelex' tablets are somewhat costly but one-sixth of a tablet dissolved in one tablespoonful of cold water will provide ample solution to treat two hundred or more selected flower buds. When applying 'gib' it is wisest not to treat more than five or six buds on each bush at first, but more may be treated on large specimens.

Gibberellic acid, whether in solid or liquid form, is completely non-toxic, so no precautions are necessary during handling, application or storage. 'Berelex' solution of gibberellic acid slowly decomposes and should be used within twenty-four hours of preparation unless stored in the bottom of a domestic refrigerator at a temperature of 35° to 40°F.

Camellias vary in their response to 'gibbing' according to variety, climate and season, so the results of 'gibbing' are quite unpredictable. In this way its use adds interest to camellia growing.

VI

Camellias in Pots and Containers

There are three kinds of gardeners who may want to grow their camellias in some kind of vessel rather than in the open ground: gardeners on chalk; those with small town gardens; and those with a balcony, roof garden, area or patio which would be embellished by a camellia in a big pot or tub.

There is an unexpected hazard in this kind of camellia culture which was made clear by some correspondence in *The Gardener's Chronicle* some years ago. A reader, and well-known amateur gardener, wrote to the paper in some indignation saying that horticultural writers and nurserymen had no right to claim that *Camellia japonica* cultivars are hardy; he himself, had had some in big pots decorating a courtyard and even in those sheltered, favourable conditions they had been killed by cold. Since there is no doubt whatever that the camellias in question were very hardy plants, the snag would appear to have been that they would not stand having their roots frozen. Yet, since they will readily stand below-zero temperatures in the open ground, that also seems questionable because they must often have their roots frozen. There is, moreover, evidence that they *will* put up even with this. Messrs D. Stewart and Son, of the Ferndown Nurseries, Wimborne, Dorset, had quantities of camellias in pots out of doors throughout the terrible winter of 1962–3. They were all frozen solid for weeks; they took no harm whatever, and (in a private communication) Messrs Stewart tell us: "Camellias are frozen with great regularity in these parts but have not suffered in consequence."

The key to this riddle is that when the entire root system becomes frozen the roots can no longer absorb moisture. The leaves continue to lose water vapour by transpiration through the stomatic pores on their undersurfaces and this moisture loss is greatly accelerated by exposure to bright sunlight and drying winds. If these conditions are prolonged then the plant dies from dessication.

The pots for camellias can be large earthenware ones, approximately the 12-inch size, decorated or otherwise; decorated earthenware or stone 'urns', half-barrels, i.e. tubs, or rectangular wooden cases. If feeding is attended to there is very little, if any, advantage in having very large containers, provided the pots are watered often enough. Whatever kind of vessel you use, it must have a number of large drainage holes in the bottom; it is easy to kill a camellia by 'drowning' the root.

The bottom of the pot or tub should be covered with 2 or 3 inches of coarse drainage material, preferably broken crocks, but large pebbles or very coarse gravel will do. You then need something to prevent the soil or compost from being leached down into the drainage and so, in time, clogging it. The traditional device is to lay a thin, fibrous turf upside-down on top of the crocks, but that is something the urban gardener may not be able to get. A few layers of very coarse sacking or hessian makes a fair substitute. It will rot away in time, but by then the soil in the container will be impacted and stable, held in a tight ball by the camellia roots.

The compost used to fill the containers to within 2 inches of the top can be John Innes No. 3 made without any lime; a lime-free, soil-less potting compost; or, if you are in a position to mix your own, a thorough mixture of something like this (details and quantities are not critical):

59

One part Irish Moss or Somerset sedge peat.
Two parts fibrous lime-free loam.
One part leaf-mould.
One part coarse silver-sand.
One handful of John Innes Base Fertilizer.

When the containers have been filled to within 2 inches of the top and thoroughly shaken down, the young camellias can be planted and made firm by hand-pressure and by very thorough watering. The soil will then go down an inch or two from the top edge of the container. It is important to tamp the compost firmly around the edges of the containers to avoid over-rapid escape of water without penetration of the soil mass.

WATERING, FEEDING AND MULCHING

Watering. We suggest that a bucket of tea-slops be left in some convenient place and water added to it, so that the camellia pots or tubs are always watered with a weak infusion of tea. However, whether you use this, or plain water (in hard-water districts some attempt should be made to catch and use rainwater rather than tap-water), the aim should be to keep the soil always moist but never very wet.

Feeding. This is important for camellias in relatively restricted pots and tubs. As soon as growth buds begin to swell, give each container half a handful of any good general fertilizer. Bone meal and hoof and horn are inclined to raise the pH because of their calcium content. Thereafter at monthly intervals, a half-handful of dried blood. Scatter the feed over the soil surface and rake it in with a miniature rake, an old comb or an old table fork. Water after feeding. An alternative is to use a liquid feed; those derived from seaweed are excellent.

Mulching. Camellias in containers benefit from mulching as much as or even more than camellias in the open border or shrubbery. The obvious material to use is moist, granulated peat. But it is possible to buy suitably treated, dried and finely divided stable or farmyard manure in bags of convenient size and quite inoffensive to handle. A half-inch layer of that with an inch of peat on top of it makes a good mulch for camellias in tubs and pots.

Frost-protection. Provided the camellias are not standing in a place exposed to dessicating and freezing east winds, we do not think it necessary to cover the whole plant; it is sufficient to protect the soil and the tub or pot. There are several ways of doing this: an easy one is to bind a 6-inch coat of straw round the pot or tub, holding it in place with a bandage of sacking or hessian. The top of the soil must, of course, also be covered. You can use plastic film instead of sacking, but the film itself has very little effect, apart from preventing loss of moisture, the temperature inside it being much the same as it is outside. But it has one use—if the whole plant be covered with a big polythene bag, bound close at the mouth, it protects the foliage against the effect of dessicating winds.

It is probable that over-potting of mature camellias is as pernicious in its effect on the bushes as on seedling camellias or rooted cuttings. There is no point, therefore, provided feeding be attended to, in using enormous containers and there may well be serious disadvantages, one of which, of course, is that of weight if you are able to move the camellias under glass for the winter.

CAMELLIAS AS GREENHOUSE AND HOUSE PLANTS

It may be the case that camellias are not very suitable for cultivation solely as house plants. It is true that they prefer shade to sunshine and respond well to a perfectly still atmosphere, and that they do well in large pots, so that in some respects they should be ideal house plants. But except

61

in houses which have very large picture-windows and so let in a great deal of light—as much as a good greenhouse in fact—the light level of a living-room and the dry atmosphere are bad for them, and unless certain precautions are taken, there will be few or no flowers.

The ideal arrangement is to grow some camellias in containers, and to move them into the house proper while they are in flower. The kind of bushes we have in mind are no bigger than, for example, the *Monsteras* and *Philodendrons* which many people have in their living-rooms.

The compost used can be the same as that used for camellias in pots and tubs out of doors and the programmes of feeding and mulching identical except that, the containers being smaller, feeding may have to be more frequent; and the air being drier, so may watering.

Two other treatments are desirable in the case of camellias grown in relatively small pots and brought into the house. The first is replacement of the top-soil every autumn. You first remove the mulch; then rake gently away at the surface doing the least possible damage to shallow roots; follow this by scooping up and throwing away the soil you have loosened to a depth of half an inch; and then replace this with fresh compost of the same kind as you used in the first place. This in due course, after thorough watering, should be covered by mulch. Such treatment would be better immediately after flowering as it would probably cause bud-drop if carried out in autumn.

The other treatment is syringing the leaves; and flowers too, when they appear. It is important in the greenhouse, but even more so in the house proper. In the greenhouse there is no problem; the water should be taken from the rainwater tank. We have found it convenient, where the catchment tank is a large one and the greenhouse electrified, to feed a supply pipe from it to a small electric pump to the outlet of which a plastic hose is fitted: this greatly reduces the labour of both watering and syringing. It is, of course, possible for those who wish to carry automation still further to fit the greenhouse with an adaptation of the mist-propagation device which will do the syringing automatically, at intervals.

It might seem to be rather an awkward business to syringe camellia bushes in the house proper, but it is much less so than would appear. If you use not an ordinary syringe but a very fine atomizer like a scent spray, so that the water comes out not as a shower of relatively large drops but as a very fine mist, and if the atomizer is managed with care, little or no water will go anywhere but onto the camellia leaves. This syringing should be done twice a day, if possible.

Over-rapid drying of the compost can be prevented by standing the pot or container in a larger and perhaps more ornamental one, which should contain a bottom layer of gravel or chippings (not limestone) to keep surplus water clear of root level. The space between the two containers should then be packed with damp moss or peat moss, or even sawdust. This will act as an absorbent which will feed surplus moisture around the container and emit a supply of humid air to the leaves of the plant.

The important role played by house plants in increasing the humidity in the excessively dry atmosphere caused by central heating is not stressed enough.

CAMELLIAS ARE ATMOSPHERIC CLEANSERS

Investigating the *Susceptibility of Plants to Hydrofluoric Acid and Sulfur Dioxide Gases* at the Boyce Thompson Institute, New York, Zimmerman and Hitchcock (1956) found that *Camellia japonica* was able to extract from the atmosphere and accumulate in its leaves abnormally large amounts of fluorine without apparent harm to the plant.

PART 2

by
Neil Treseder

VII

Some Camellia Recollections

'I should like to think that this chapter would encourage the planting of ten thousand camellias, in small simple gardens as well as grand ones. For these are not simply plants for the rich man's greenhouse, as used to be supposed; they are plants for Everyman.' Thus, in 1947, wrote my old friend the late Will Arnold-Forster in his well-known book *Shrubs for the Milder Counties*. I remember reading and helping to correct his original manuscript, for it inspired me, and doubtless many others, to propagate, grow, plant and promote the sale of many thousands of these beautiful evergreen shrubs. Surely there could be no finer epitaph to such a great gardener, artist and author.

In his garden at 'Eagles' Nest', Zennor, perched high on the open Cornish moorland beside the coastal road between St Ives and Land's End, Arnold-Forster grew many kinds of camellias to perfection in two narrow borders flanked by low stone walls, over the top of which one looked out across the open sea to the Isles of Scilly. Here he proved, beyond any doubt, that camellias will tolerate much wind, though they dislike draught. These camellias continued to flourish after their growth overtopped the shelter of the walls and their upper parts became exposed to the exaggerated fury of Atlantic gales. His book has long been out of print and it is questionable whether anyone will ever undertake the task of revising it and bringing it up to date. I therefore hope that this joint effort will inspire many more would-be gardeners to plant camellias.

But before I go on to write about camellias themselves, I must say a little about the origins of my connection with them.

Our Truro nurseries were founded by my great-grand-father in 1830. My grandfather emigrated to Australia with two of his brothers in 1860 and they were propagating and growing camellias over a century ago when they had nurseries at Ashfield, near Sydney, known as Camellia Grove, where they traded under the name of Treseder Bros.

My father was born at Camellia Grove, and often told me how he and his brothers used to climb down from their bedroom window through a camellia tree which was growing against the wall of the house. He also told me how they assisted in collecting specimens of Australian Tree Ferns (*Dicksonia antarctica*) from the Blue Mountains and packing them for despatch to such favoured Cornish gardens as Bosahan, Caerhays, Trengwainton and Trewidden, where many fine specimens survive to this day.

My grandfather did much evangelical work among the Australian aborigines in the course of which he travelled widely, visiting many outlying islands. In an endeavour to help the inhabitants he started a world-wide trade in their native seeds, bartering building materials and household utensils for seed of the Norfolk Island Pine (*Araucaria excelsa*) and the Lord Howe Palms (*Howea belmoriana* and *H. forsteriana*), the latter being better known as Kentia Palms. All of these plants became as popular as the universal Aspidistra as house plants in Victorian times. I still possess copies of some of the correspondence relating to this trade, with details of the manner in which the seeds were packed in sealed tins for export, not only to pot-plant growers and seedsmen in Great Britain, but also in Europe and America.

About 1950 I became the proud possessor of one of the scarce copies of *Camellia Quest* by the well-known Australian camellia authority, Professor E. G. Waterhouse. Imagine my delight when I came across the following under the heading 'Various Australian Seedlings': ' *"Winter Cheer"* a seedling found growing at the foot of *"Tricolor"* at Treseder's old nursery, Alt Street, Ashfield, and named by Mr A. O. Ellison. It is probably a *"Tricolor"* seedling. A large, showy, semi-double rosy-crimson.' The Australian variety 'Thomas Treseder', a large semi-double, salmon-red, veined rose, was named after one of my great-uncles and has recently been introduced into our camellia stock from propagating material supplied by the Melbourne Botanic Gardens.

In 1898 my grandfather returned to Cornwall to revive his father's nursery business at Truro, the lease of which had meantime passed temporarily into other hands. He was followed in 1900 by my Australian-born parents and later by a second son. It would appear that, in the ensuing years they turned their artistic talents to the planning and landscaping of gardens, doubtless finding this more remunerative than the propagation of such ornamental plants as camellias, which were still generally considered only fit for greenhouse and conservatory cultivation, the era of the camellia as a hardy garden plant being yet to come. Thus for over half a century there was a lapse in the propagation and cultivation of camellias in any quantity in our nurseries, whilst most of our saleable stock was imported each autumn from specialist growers in France and Belgium.

The second wave of popularity for camellias began in about 1948, when Britain was gradually recovering from wartime shortages and restrictions in motoring and travelling abroad. This time they were not sought after exclusively as conservatory and greenhouse plants, as they were in Victorian times, but as hardy evergreen shrubs for garden ornament. The introduction of mist-propagation techniques in the early 1950s provided nurserymen with the ideal method of modern camellia production. I only hope that the spread of this boon into the hands of a multitude of amateur gardeners will not produce such an excessive quantity of camellias that the demand for plants will decline to the extent that professional growers will find them no longer profitable. Maybe the writing is already appearing on the wall, for such a state of affairs might well precipitate a rapid decline in camellia culture in Britain. If nurserymen were forced to reduce their stocks of these plants they would be very wary about accepting new introductions for propagation and distribution, and many an outstanding new variety might be allowed to remain with the raiser without a chance of becoming known to the gardening public at large.

Gardening has become the only art in which the expert is expected to impart the knowledge, which he has gained from long experience, to the casual enquirer without recompense. It is a way of life, a vocation rather than a profession, and I cannot help wondering whether this is a good thing. It is human nature to value most what is costly, no matter whether it be a service or the acquisition of an expensive *objet d'art*.

Gardening is an ageless occupation, a way of life which keeps one fit and youthful in body and mind. Once, when my grandfather was admonished by a foreman for walking round the nursery in pouring rain at the age of eighty he exclaimed: 'My good man, Moses didn't begin his great work until he was eighty!'

I am often asked, 'Could I grow camellias in my garden?' I am quite certain that in most cases the answer could be 'Yes'. Although camellias prefer a lime-free soil, they are not as intolerant of lime as are rhododendrons, azaleas, kalmias, pieris, pernettyas and most summer-flowering heaths. I know of many instances where they survive in quite alkaline soils (with a pH of 8 and over) where they have ample shade and a soil rich in decomposing vegetation or humus which does not become too dry in summer.

It is almost certain that there would be many more ancient specimens of camellia surviving in gardens today if they had not been looked upon in the past as half-hardy plants requiring the hottest and driest part of the garden. They were too often planted against south- or west-facing walls where they not only suffered from soil adulterated by the weathering of mortar-jointed brick and stone work, but their root systems often had to compete with those of many other plants, often bedding kinds, the replanting of which entailed a thorough digging over of the surrounding soil at least twice a year. Little wonder, then, that few of them survived, their failure doubtless assumed due to lack of hardiness.

Camellias are most resentful of root disturbance once they become established. Consequently a border which is dug over at regular intervals, perhaps to accommodate bulbs or seasonal bedding plants, is just not their 'cup of tea'. Speaking of tea reminds me that they are, as the reader already knows, first cousins of the commercial Tea Plant *Camellia theifera,* and it is interesting to notice how sickly camellias respond to regular waterings with spent tea and tea leaves. It is just like providing them with their own leaf mould, a perfectly natural top dressing which they will produce themselves once they become fully established. So, if you have any camellias in your garden which are sickly in appearance or which do not flower regularly, try saving all your spent tea and tea leaves and water your plants with it two or three times a week, at any rate from April to the end of August. You will be surprised to see the effect of such a tonic.

I am well aware that such advice sounds like some old wives' tale. It may have originated as such, for the custom of watering pot plants with spent tea is a regular practice among cottage gardeners in many rural areas. So, if you have camellias in other than ideal conditions, please do not throw away this most useful form of domestic waste, or, if you drink coffee, use your waste coffee and coffee grounds instead. Swill your tea or coffee pot into a bucket kept specially for the purpose and give it to your camellias, azaleas, rhododendrons, summer-flowering heaths and blue hydrangeas. The improvement in their growth and blossom will be most rewarding, for not only will you be irrigating them in dry weather, but you will be maintaining a constant supply of mildly acid soil moisture which will gradually neutralize any excess of lime close to their roots. Garden owners requiring more of this waste material than is available from their own households should track down the vast amounts thrown away by hotels, cafés, restaurants, schools and tea meetings at church and village halls, Women's Institutes and the like.

Although camellias will tolerate open, sunny situations they seem to prefer partial or complete shade. They will withstand the drip of overhanging trees better than any other evergreen shrub, and there is no better ornamental for a north-facing border, provided it is not too exposed to icy winds. Camellias prefer a medium to heavy soil which does not dry out too quickly. Lighter soils should have liberal quantities of old manure, or moist granulated peat, forked in prior to planting and the very minimum of subsequent cultivations. Surrounding weed growth should be kept down by hand weeding, very shallow hoeings, or better still by mulching; but never dig in these top dressings. Modern non-residual herbicides, such as paraquat, are excellent in careful hands, but will burn any leaves which are accidentally contaminated. They are the most important contribution of modern science to garden maintenance.

There are, of course, many gardens where the soil is so alkaline that the cultivation of camellias, without special precautions, is quite out of the question. Large pots, tubs, old oil drums and even polythene sacks may be sunk to within an inch or so of the surface in any shaded and sheltered corner, prior to filling firmly with imported lime-free soil liberally dressed with peat, then planted with camellias and watered as often as possible with spent tea and tea leaves as described above. Carefully follow the planting instructions and avoid deep planting. The containers must, of course, have adequate drainage holes.

It is possible to transplant camellias of considerable age and size if they are correctly treated and given suitable after-care. Edward Hyams has already touched on this subject but some personal experiences may be of interest. I once successfully transferred three plants known to be eighty years old from the borders of a dried-out conservatory during a heat-wave in mid-May. They had already completed their first growth flush and could scarcely have been in a less promising state, but they were good varieties which were in immediate danger of destruction through possible building development and I was allowed only twenty-four hours to remove them. I realized that it would be fatal to lift them as they were, so I made a snap decision and proceeded as follows.

First, my assistant David Knuckey, who later spent two years as a student at Wisley before becoming our propagator, helped me to spur back all side branches flush with the main trunks so that we were left with a leafless framework of older branches.

The soil was like powder, so dry that water simply ran off it, so they had to be lifted with completely bare roots and scarcely a trace of fibre. As soon as we got them back to the nursery we laid them in the old mill leat which runs along our lower boundary whilst three pits were excavated in the floor of an old sunken fern house and half filled with a mixture of lime-free loam, old manure, peat and sand, with several handfuls of a balanced fertilizer. The house had a

73

three-quarter span roof and they were planted against the back south-facing wall, taking care to set them at the same depth as before and thoroughly shaking them to ensure that the soil settled around their roots without any air pockets before it was tamped and trodden tight.

We then procured three 5-gallon oil drums from which the tops were removed, burnt out all traces of oil over a straw fire, before punching a central hole in the bottom of each with a 6-inch nail and fixing thick wire handles to their rims.

One of these was hung above each of the skeletonized camellias, and then we proceeded to tie strands of thick jute fillis twine to the base of each branch, binding them in tight spirals upwards, and passing the ends into the holes made in the bottoms of the drums where they were knotted together. The drums were then filled with water, the strands of twine and the branches saturated with a hose and the plants copiously flooded in.

The operation was completed by fastening hessian blinds to the glass on the south side of the house and placing a bucket of water and a syringe at the foot of each camellia. It was the thirteenth of May, but it wasn't Friday and I kept my fingers crossed.

In those days the fern house was a short cut from the old packing shed to the even older office. Everyone was now encouraged to pass through the house *en route* and give each of the plants a squirt, since the weather was so hot by day that the combined capillary and gravitational flow of water down the strands tended to evaporate in transit. In addition, the oil drums and water buckets were kept topped up from a nearby hose, an operation combining a thorough sousing of their trunks and branches. We could use all the water we could pump, thanks to the efforts of the workmen who built the leat way back in 1648. I knew that if we could keep their bark cool and turgid they had a good chance of survival.

The pessimists declared our efforts a waste of time and, even when the branches began to burgeon with clusters of growth buds six weeks later these were declared 'proud growth which would come to nothing'.

By September the ends of their branches were so densely clothed with young shoots that I thought it prudent to thin them. I carefully excised about a third from each plant and passed them on to our propagator as cuttings. In March I removed about half of the remainder, arguing that over-crowded growths would provide hiding places for mealy bugs and scale insects and that it was better to divert the spring flow of sap into fewer, well-placed shoots. My contention proved correct, for they all survived and flourished.

'Altheaflora' proceeded to flower so freely that it has always been a great temptation to cut it too harshly for the March flower shows. We nearly over-did it one year and I thought that the tree was beginning to fail. Next winter I removed all of the flower buds myself to give it a well-earned rest and a chance to recuperate.

'Optima' grew away with extraordinary vigour so that soon it had insufficient headroom. It was in the shadier end of the house in the angle of the end wall, which continued up to roof level, being the back of an adjacent shed. Consequently it has never flowered as freely as 'Altheaflora' but it did give rise to a fine salmon-pink branch sport which I later named 'Wally Abbiss' after a close friend, the late Henry Walter Abbiss, who was very well known in horticultural circles, having been County Horticultural Advisor for Cornwall for over thirty years and largely responsible for many important innovations in the county's horticultural industry.

The third plant was 'Preston Rose', the foliage of which was variegated with virus infection at the start and which consequently made much slower progress than the others. Whilst useless as a mother plant I did not like to destroy it for sentimental reasons, so it was later replanted against the

15-foot north face of our wall garden, a brick enclosure of about one third of an acre of unknown age but still in an excellent state of preservation.

I have since repeated this type of transplanting where regular spraying was impracticable: instead I had the branches covered with a thick coating of wet sphagnum moss, bound on wreath-frame fashion with spiralled twine, before covering the ground with a deep layer of litter to keep the roots cool and moist.

On another occasion I was asked to arrange the transplanting of a fifty-year-old camellia from one part of a garden to another because it was in the way of a proposed new building. This was quite a different problem, because it was in January, about the best time for such an operation since the bush was still dormant. It was a fine specimen of 'Rubescens Major', about 10 feet high by as much across.

Whilst my staff were busy preparing a pit to accommodate its root ball I busied myself with a secateurs. Worming my way between the branches I proceeded to cut out all weaker ones flush with the trunk before working among the main branches in the same manner. In this way I removed quite one third of the total foliage and then proceeded to shorten the longest of the remaining branches before removing the flower buds on those retained.

An incline about 4 feet wide was then excavated towards the centre of the bush to accommodate an earth scoop which we used as a sleigh. The roots were cut round vertically to form a large root-ball, the earth scoop was placed at the foot of the incline, covered with a large sheet of thick sacking, then the camellia was tipped over onto it and the hessian wrap secured around the root-ball with ropes.

Because of risks of damage to lawns and borders it was not possible to mechanize the haulage across the garden, so a strong rope was attached to the main trunk and the plant heaved along in easy stages with a block and tackle.

This 'Rubescens Major' flowered freely fourteen months later, by which time it was difficult to believe that it had ever been moved.

The lessons are: Never play clever and think that you can get away with transplanting a large evergreen, other than a rhododendron, without reducing its leafage considerably. Your plant may look well enough until April or May and then show very sudden distress as soon as warm, dry weather sets in. It may then be too late to try to save it unless all the branches are cut back to rid it of its foliage, a much more drastic treatment than was necessary in the beginning.

Secondly, plant firmly and at the correct depth, taking care to retamp the soil round the roots when it begins to dry and shrink, then water copiously and apply a mulch of litter to keep the roots cool and moist.

Thirdly, stake your plant securely even if it has a very heavy root-ball. Drive a really stout stake diagonally from the centre of the trunk away from the root-ball in the same direction as the prevailing wind and carefully band the area of contact between trunk and stake before tying, to prevent chafing in windy weather.

Fourthly, remember that overhead irrigation in late evening or overnight is much more beneficial than 'car-washing' the ground beneath the bush with a high pressure hose.

Fifthly, avoid wetting the foliage in hot, sunny weather if the roots are dry, since this may cause leaf-scorch. Provided the roots are moist there is no risk of this trouble developing, however hot the sun.

CAMELLIAS AND EXPOSURE-RESISTANCE

A few days after one Christmas I was delighted to come across a bush of *C. japonica* 'Gloire de Nantes' commencing

77

to flower in an exposed garden alongside a lane leading to a Cornish clifftop. Situated close to the seaward face of a low concrete wall, where wind velocities would be increased by this artificial obstruction, the plant had withstood the onslaught of salt-laden gales for probably twenty years. The wind had restricted its annual growth to 2 or 3 inches, so that it had formed a very tight and compact bush which was densely studded with flower buds, some of which had already opened to bright rose, semi-double blossoms.

Recalling that, in Japan, the natural distribution of the native camellia extends from the mountain slopes to the cliff tops overlooking the Sea of Japan, I am sure that they should be tried more daringly in coastal gardens here, where the soil has not become over-adulterated with calcareous sea sand, the high lime content of which is derived from pulverized seashells. One should, of course, bear in mind that cliff-top gardens do not have to contend with so much wind-blown salt as those which are situated nearer beach-level, or in valleys sloping down to the sea, up which the wind drives spray and spume with terrific violence whenever there is an on-shore gale.

If you have a garden in such an exposed environment, be sure to delay the planting of all evergreen trees and shrubs until late spring or early summer, so that they can become established with little risk of immediate storm damage and adapt themselves to the change of climate and environment before the autumn gales return. Try camellias with tough, leathery leaves which are not of abnormal size and avoid those with white flowers which readily bruise and turn brown in wind, rain or hail. For obvious reasons it is safer to plant a variety such as 'Gloire de Nantes', which opens its flower buds in prolonged succession, rather than one which opens all its flowers in a spectacular display, so readily damaged or destroyed by a sudden gale.

Remember, too, that camellias are surface-rooting and

that wind dries the soil far more rapidly than does hot sunshine. Consequently be lavish with peat or old manure, thoroughly incorporating it with the soil prior to planting, and adding more each year as a top dressing before dry weather sets in. If the wind tends to blow the mulch away, retain it with a collar of wire netting some 6 inches high and not less than 3 feet in diameter. Avoid piling the mulch up around the main stem or trunk and remember that the vital feeding roots usually extend outwards to the limit of the branches where they can take advantage of leaf drip from dew, mist and light rain.

SOME OUTSTANDING CAMELLIAS

With such a diversity of colour, flower form and growth habit to choose from, the selection of varieties is not always easy. I am often asked which is my favourite camellia. I like them all so much that I have never quite made up my mind.

When selecting a range of camellias for my own garden I would give careful consideration to securing as long a succession of bloom as possible. Bear in mind that, whereas the camellia plant is remarkably frost-hardy, the fully open flowers are susceptible to frost damage and the white varieties particularly so. Red flowers absorb and retain heat, which may be why they are less likely to be affected. They will usually stand up to 10 degrees of frost if screened from early morning sun.

It is obvious that a camellia which opens all its blossoms in one flush, whilst creating a sensational garden display, carries all its eggs in one basket. Its beauty is liable to disappear overnight from a few degrees of frost, especially if the flowers are white or the plant is exposed to early morning sunlight.

I think that I would start my camellia season with *Camel-*

79

lia sasanqua 'Narumigata'. This vigorous and erect growing camellia often masquerades in nurseries under *C. oleifera.* We have already described how it differs from the true *oleifera,* which has smaller flowers and dull, matt-surfaced leaves. The flowers of 'Narumigata' have carmine-purple tinted buds which open to single white flowers resembling Christmas Roses, with an evasive, heavy fragrance. Often commencing to bloom in late October it will sometimes extend its flower period into early January. Its long slender branches make it ideal for wall training, and it appears to be equally at home on any wall aspect. The flowers, lasting longest in almost complete shade, are remarkably frost-resistant for a white variety.

The *sasanquas* are a distinct race of camellias, not all of which are autumn-flowering. The *hiemalis* varieties flower in mid-winter and the *vernalis* varieties in the spring. All of them are more or less fragrant, most have single flowers, but there are also semi-double and double varieties, especially of the *vernalis* types. 'Crimson King' (*sasanqua*) has single crimson flowers in autumn, whilst 'Hiryu' (*hiemalis*) is a semi-double crimson, winter-flowering variety. One of the most distinctive of the *vernalis* varieties is 'Dawn', which has leaves conspicuously blotched cream, and bears fragrant, semi-double white flowers in spring which are sometimes faintly flushed with pink.

Some authorities list *C. x vernalis* as a hybrid between *C. japonica* and *C. sasanqua.* Apparently neither *C. hiemalis* nor *C. vernalis* have been found in the wild, so they may be both of hybrid origin.

One of the earliest of the *japonica* varieties is the double white 'Nobilissima'. This is an erect grower which flowers with such continuity that the open blossoms are almost certain to be frosted at some period during its flowering. These damaged blossoms tend to remain on the branches for some time, after turning a parchment yellow colour which I find not unattractive. The rose-pink, semi-double 'Gloire de Nantes' is earlier still. Because these varieties continue to flower right through winter they really deserve wall protection, but face them west or north rather than south or east, for hot sun on frosted or dew-laden flowers may spoil them.

Perhaps the most reliable of all camellias is 'Adolphe Audusson'. This robust, erect-growing cultivar usually opens its large, semi-double scarlet blossoms in early March, in some seasons much earlier, sometimes turning rosy red in warm, dry weather. The large central bosses of yellow stamens show up from a considerable distance and seem to illuminate the flowers. Its tough, polished foliage is well spaced along stout, erect branches and the flowers are re-markably weatherproof. It is, without doubt, the most popular of the older Japonica cultivars but it is now being strongly challenged by *C. x williamsii* 'Donation', which produces large semi-double silvery pink blossoms in greater profusion.

Marriages between varieties of the Japanese *Camellia japonica* and the Chinese species *saluenensis,* originally per-formed at Caerhays in Cornwall prior to 1930 and giving rise to the famous Williamsii Hybrids, have done more than anything else to encourage the planting of camellias as hardy garden plants. 'J.C. Williams' and Donation' are among the best-known *C. x williamsii* cultivars at the present time. However, I think that, in climates less suited to camellias than that of Cornwall, 'Adolphe Audusson' will hold its popularity, especially for the amateur's first venture into camelliadom. It will certainly grow in soil conditions and exposures likely to prove fatal to 'Donation', though the Williamsii Hybrids flower more reliably in northern lati-tudes where 'Adolphe Audusson' along with other Japonica camellias find the summer temperatures too low for flower-bud initiation.

81

I would certainly include a good selection of these Williamsii Hybrids, particularly 'J. C. Williams', with its prolonged succession of pale pink, dog-rose flowers; the more erect-growing 'St Ewe' of richer hue, and 'November Pink', which sometimes commences to blossom in October and carries on for five or six months into the spring.

'Elegans' (Chandleri Elegans) is another old Japonica variety which will always remain popular on account of its very large rosy-pink flowers with anemone centres. It is interesting to note that older plants lose the anemone form of their flowers, which tend to become more paeony-form in appearance, the difference in size between inner and outer petals becoming less pronounced.

Similar in shape is 'Altheaflora', which has flowers of the richest crimson-scarlet. There is a giant form of this variety which opens its immense scarlet flowers from almost spherical buds. I have named it 'Altheaflora Gigantea' since its origin and identity are obscure. It received an Award of Merit from the Royal Horticultural Society on 21 February 1967. I am indebted to Mrs S. Williams of Scorrier House for allowing me to propagate and distribute this magnificent, almost voluptuous camellia. My grandfather received his early training in the gardens of Scorrier House. I often wonder if this camellia was growing in the greenhouse over a century ago, or could it be an Australian variety which he sent over from his Camellia Grove Nursery at Ashfield near Sydney a few years later? Could this be related to the Waratah Camellia of New South Wales?

One of the most vivid of all camellias is 'Arejishi', which produces precocious flowers of crimson-scarlet. The petals are usually notched and frilled to give the flowers a carnation-like resemblance. The leaves are pendulous and quite distinct in shape and texture, being abnormally long and tapering evenly to their points. The venation is conspicuously raised and reticulate, and the plant has an open, bushy habit.

The well-known Japanese plantsman Mr K. Wada of Hakoneya Nurseries, Yokohama, tells me the most interesting camellias in Japan are of the Wabisuke group. Some are probably variations of *Camellia japonica* but the others have ovaries densely hairy. They seem to suggest *saluenensis* blood, or *pitardii* blood. 'Tarokaja' is one of the group obviously, and has salmon-pink funnel-shaped flowers, the colour generally seen in *C. saluenensis*.

These Wabisuke Camellias are usually of compact, erect habit with lustreless, dark green leaves and small, single, trumpet-shaped blossoms. Japanese botanists have suggested that they are hybrids of *C. reticulata,* but this seems most improbable. They are reputed to have originated in China and are more likely to be hybrids between *C. japonica* and *C. sinensis.* They are usually referred to as *C. wabiske,* whilst the name 'Wabisuke' is used to denote the various cultivars. The form most usually met with in British gardens is 'Beni-Wabisuke', which has small, bright red trumpets and red stamen filaments. It appears to be very similar to the cultivar 'Kimberley' of Cornish gardens, the leaves of which are darker and glossier with pronounced, impressed, reticulate venations and denticulate margins. 'Momoiro-Wabisuke' has soft pink trumpets closely resembling the supposed Japonica cultivar 'Migali'. 'Kocho-Wabisuke' has red trumpet flowers flecked and spotted white. 'Shiro-Wabisuke' has pure white flowers often opening wider than those of other forms.

A camellia cultivar growing in several English gardens under the name 'Migali' (at Dartington Hall in Devon and also at Trewidden in Cornwall) presents a poser. It is clearly not a Japonica since it has hairy ovaries. Mr K. Wada examined young plants of this in our nursery and thought that it looked like one of the mysterious Wabisuke camellias. It certainly resembles 'Momoiro-Wabisuke', but the flowers are larger and tend to open flat instead of being small and campanulate. It could be, of course, of the same parentage

as the modern Williamsii hybrids, supposing that it originated in China where camellias have been hybridized and
cultivated since time immemorial.

Dr Siro Kitamura, of the University of Kyoto, tells us
that the Wabisuke Camellias became very popular in Japan
between 1650 and 1675, to be followed a century later by the
Higo varieties of *C. japonica,* which were bred for their
splayed contrasting stamens.

The Japanese also like to grow Bonsai camellias. These are
plants of restricted vigour and grotesque habit, created by
skilled Japanese craftsmen who graft selected varieties onto
the twisted roots of Snow Camellias after these have been
successfully pot-established. Bonsai camellias make very little
annual growth but flower freely and enable their owner
to admire the beauty of their leaves and blossoms at close
range, indoors, for a much longer period than is possible
with cut material. In Japan, Bonsai Higo camellias are
looked upon as family heirlooms.

Higo camellias are a race of Japanese garden varieties
bred in the old province of Higo (pronounced Hee-go),
now known as Kumamoto Prefecture on Kyushu Island. Most
Higo camellias have thick, rounded, broad-petalled, single
or semi-double flowers. They have conspicuously splayed
stamens, reminiscent of those of the apricot, but varying in
colour from white to soft pink or pale yellow. Higo camellias
are usually dwarf and prostrate, a characteristic probably
inherited from the Snow Camellia.

These Higo camellias have been bred and selected by a
brotherhood of camellia fanatics known as the 'Hanaren',
whose creed is that, as the heart of the samurai (warrior) is
to his body, so are the stamens of a camellia to the flower.
They consider that a camellia should display not less than
one hundred stamens to qualify as a Higo variety. The
Hanaren guard their plants with such tenacity that they
are often referred to as 'mokkosu'—the stubborn ones. They

84

rarely, if ever, part with plants or propagating material even to their closest relations.

It is interesting to recall that, whereas the main commercial importance of the genus camellia lies in the production of tea from the leaves and young shoots of *C. sinensis,* the Japanese have always regarded camellias as the traditional source of a widely used vegetable oil which they express from its seeds. It is used in cosmetics and cooking. The long dark tresses of their womenfolk were dressed with camellia oil and those Japanese who attained the ripe age of ninety, celebrated what is known as the 'age of the camellia'.

Camellia flowers had various traditional significances in old Japan, where the single forms were favoured on account of their prominent golden stamens. The samurai, warrior knights of a bygone era, superstitiously regarded the fall of a camellia blossom as an ill omen.

In Europe camellia blossoms became romanticized about 1850 when the young Alexandre Dumas wrote *La Dame aux Camélias.* In it he described how a beautiful courtesan named Marguerite Gautier 'invariably had three things with her on the ledge of her second-floor box; her opera-glass, a bag of sweets and a bouquet of camellias. For twenty-five days of the month the camellias were white, and for five they were red; no one ever seemed to realize the reason for this change in colour, which I mention though I cannot explain it; it was noticed by her friends and by the habitués of the theatres to which she often went. She was never seen with any flowers but camellias. At the florist's, Madam Barjons, she had come to be called "the Lady of the Camellias", and the name stuck.' How very naive!

VIII

Camellia Japonica

As we have written, this species embraces practically all of the camellia varieties grown in Europe and America until quite recent times.

The bold, tough, glossy foliage varies, according to variety, from under 2 to over 6 inches in length. The leaf shapes and margins vary considerably. Thus the Fishtail camellia, *C. japonica* 'Kingyo-Tsubaki', has peculiar split and twisted ends to its leaves, whilst 'Arejishi' has extra long, pointed leaves with deep indentations and raised veins reminiscent of *C. reticulata*.

An experienced camellia grower can recognize many varieties of *Camellia japonica* from their leaves, and there is no doubt that the specialist can do so for a considerable number of cultivars with a remarkable degree of accuracy.

One autumn I was offered propagating material from a 20-foot high camellia growing against the south wall of a Cornish mansion, which had to be regularly pruned because it overgrew the windows each summer. The owner assured me that it was 'Mathotiana Alba', but I knew immediately that it was in fact another double white cultivar, 'Alba Plena', which bears narrower, slightly twisted leaves of quite different appearance. In fact I would have known by the feel of the leaves had I been blindfolded.

The foliage of *Camellia japonica* lasts extremely well when cut and the glossy surface reflects artificial light in a most attractive manner. As a rule only mature plants which have been severely pruned will provide the long straight shoots sought after by the florist. These are usually three or more years old by the time they become marketable, so it is little wonder that camellia foliage remains scarce and costly. Whereas most of the camellia foliage marketed is taken from old severely pruned trees (usually those with inferior blossoms), one famous Cornish garden grows its own particular strain of *Camellia japonica* for commercial cut foliage. This has the single red flowers of the original species but the foliage is quite remarkable, being of below-average size, well spaced on the branches and of the darkest green imaginable, with such a glossy surface as to appear as if it had been laquered. Little wonder that it fetches such a high price, but would-be growers of camellia foliage should beware. Even under the most sheltered woodland conditions it takes at least ten years before a plant makes sufficient growth for marketing and afterwards only during each second or third winter is it fit to be cut.

The skilled flower arranger, however, is often more interested in quite a different type of camellia growth, seeking long, arching branches from the sides and base of camellia bushes especially for pedestal arrangements, and stunted, twiggy shoots for Ikebana creations.

Some cultivars of *Camellia japonica*, notably 'Imbricata Rubra', bear long, slender shoots with large, well-spaced leaves sometimes attractively blotched and flushed creamy yellow. Some authorities consider this condition to be caused by a virus, but as it often occurs only on one side of a bush, I am inclined to think that it is sometimes physiological and probably due to an excess or deficiency of some trace element in the soil round the roots on the opposite side of the bush.

In the camellia-growing states of America the name 'Japonica' is used as gardening slang for camellia in the same way as it is often used in Britain for the Japanese Quince (*Chaenomeles,* or *Cydonia japonica*). There are, of course, a great many other native Japanese plants which bear the same latinized adjective to designate their origin, and it is not surprising that such slang usage can cause considerable confusion. For example, I remember an occasion some years ago when a gardening acquaintance telephoned me late one evening to enquire whether I could possibly have two dozen 'Japonica' stocks ready for him to collect in the morning as he had just received scions of several new varieties from America. I did not then appreciate that he had been reading American camellia publications in which this term was used to the extent that he had assumed that it was a recognized form of international plant jargon. Imagine his reaction when he saw the naked and spindly *Chaenomeles* seedlings which I had prepared for him to collect when he called next day expecting to find two-year pot-grown camellias.

Many of the varieties still popular today originated centuries ago in China and Japan. They were often renamed on introduction into the West either because their labelling was illegible or their oriental names were unintelligible. Scores of other varieties were raised by British and Continental breeders during the great vogue for camellias as greenhouse plants in Victorian times, when new varieties fetched fantastically high prices, even at present-day standards.

There is a tremendously wide range of flower colours and forms, some varieties opening their blooms in long succession from as early as mid-December until late April (e.g. 'Nobilissima', double white, and 'Gloire de Nantes', semi-double rosy-red) whilst others open all their blooms in one brief but more sensational display (e.g. 'Donation', semi-double silvery-pink, 'Sylva', single crimson, and 'Donckelarii', semi-double red).

The growth habit of camellias varies to an extent that makes it possible and prudent to select varieties according to the space available for the spread and the height to which they may be desired to grow. The extremes in growth habit include 'Lady Clare', with large semi-double rose-pink flowers, which may well have a spread of three or four times its height, and the most popular of all, *Camellia japonica* 'Adolphe Audusson', a vigorous and erect growing variety with large semi-double crimson-scarlet flowers displaying conspicuous bosses of golden stamens. This is probably one of the easiest camellias to grow. I have often seen it established in soils and environments where I would not have risked such a valuable plant.

Another very erect-growing variety is 'Optima', a cultivar ideally suitable for borders and gardens where space is at a premium. It has rather unusual rose-form to peony-form flowers of bright pink, streaked with carmine, which are clustered very close to erect-growing stems, almost as if they had been wired on by a florist.

I will now describe more fully some of the *C. japonica* cultivars already mentioned, together with others which I consider to be outstanding. For ease of reference these are arranged in alphabetical sequence. I grow over two hundred varieties and my selection is not a random one. Most of the varieties are in general circulation at the present time, in other words, they are available from most camellia growers in the United Kingdom and America.

To make these descriptions more readily understood I will begin the list with details of their flower classifications.

The various flower forms of camellia are divided into six, internationally accepted, classes for the purpose of identification and flower show competitions as follows:

Class 1: SINGLE: one row of not over eight petals.
Examples: 'Sylva', bright red; 'Amabilis', white.
Class 2: SEMI-DOUBLE: Two or more rows of regular, loose or irregular petals, conspicuous stamens.
Examples: 'Adolphe Audusson', crimson-scarlet; 'Latifolia', rosy-red.

89

Class 3:   ANEMONE FORM: One or more rows of large outer petals lying flat or undulating, the centre a convex mass of intermingled petaloids and stamens.

           Examples: 'Anemonaeflora', light, rosy-red; 'Altheaflora', vivid crimson-scarlet.

Class 4:   PEONY FORM: A deep, rounded flower, with loose petals and intermingled stamens, varying to a convex mass of mixed petals, petaloids and stamens, or irregular petals never showing stamens, of fully double form.

           Examples: 'Arejishi', crimson-scarlet; 'Nobilissima', white; 'Optima', blush-pink flecked carmine.

Class 5:   ROSE FORM DOUBLE: Imbricated (overlapping) petals, showing stamens in a concave centre when fully opened.

           Examples: 'Mathotiana', deep crimson; 'Mme Lebois', light red; 'Thomas Treseder', salmon-red veined rose.

Class 6:   FORMAL DOUBLE: Fully imbricated with many rows of petals never showing stamens.

           Examples: 'Alba Plena', white; 'Imbricata Rubra', light red; 'Rubescens Major', bright rose.

           'Ranunculus Form' is the term sometimes applied to formal doubles which have incurved petals. e.g. 'Compte de Boutourlin' and 'Reine de Beautés'.

To supplement these floral classifications the uninitiated may require definitions for some of the terms used frequently in describing these camellias. These are explained elsewhere in this book but we repeat them here for the benefit of the more casual reader.

Branch Sport. Some camellias tend to produce occasional shoots with flowers of a different form or colour. Where such a variation persists it is possible to remove all or part

90

of the 'sported' branch and propagate it as a distinct variety, either by grafting it onto a separate root stock, or by rooting it from cuttings.

Cultivar Name. The special name (varietal designation) given to a cultivated variety (cultivar) ; e.g. 'Adolphe Audusson' is a cultivar of *Camellia japonica.*

Imbricated is the botanical term applied to flowers with many rows of petals overlapping evenly, like tiles, in regular, concentric rows.

Petaloids. Modified stamens resembling narrow strap-like petals. These form the central boss in anemone-form camellia blooms. They are usually arranged in a twisted cluster and may be intermingled with true anther-bearing stamens.

Reticulate. The term applied to leaves or petals with pronounced net-like vein patterns. *Camellia reticulata* was so named because of the pronounced reticulation impressed into the upper surfaces of the leaves of 'Captain Rawes', which was the first form examined by Western botanists.

A SELECTION OF CAMELLIA JAPONICA CULTIVARS

'ADOLPHE AUDUSSON'. We have already given this well-known variety the highest praise. It combines the good qualities of hardiness and vigour with bold, brightly coloured, semi-double blossoms of bright crimson-scarlet which have conspicuous bosses of yellow stamens. In hot weather the flowers sometimes fade to rosy-red. The foliage is boldly rounded and of extra heavy texture with highly polished upper surfaces and pronounced downward curved edges. The growth is vigorous and erect. It was raised in the latter part of the nineteenth century by a French nurseryman of that name from Angers and was introduced by the camellia specialists Guichard Souers of Nantes.

'ALBA PLENA'. A compact slow-growing bush; the small, dark green, twisted leaves are lustreless with conspicuously impressed veins. The immaculately white flowers are formal double, displaying the symmetrical overlapping of petals known as 'imbricated'. They open in long succession, often from January to April, especially under glass or against a sheltered wall. Like all white camellias, the open flowers are liable to frost and wind damage, and, unfortunately, these tend to remain and disfigure the bush. However, the manner in which it holds its blossoms without dropping makes it an ideal cut-flower variety.

'Fimbriata' is a branch sport of 'Alba Plena' with fringed petals and is often listed as 'Fimbriata Alba'.

'AREJISHI'. A very distinct, bushy variety readily recognizable by its extra long and narrow, tapering, light green leaves, with conspicuously raised veins. The flowers, which often open extra early, are bright crimson-scarlet and usually peony-form. The variety 'Heckla' appears to be almost identical except that the habit is more open and erect and the flowers are later. Petiolar hairs on the young leaf stalks indicate that it owes its origin to the Snow Camellia (*C. rusticana*). 'Arejishi Variegated' is a salmon-pink branch sport often marbled white.

'CONTESSA LAVINIA MAGGI' forms a rounded, spreading bush with broad, leathery foliage. The large formal double to rose-form flowers are flecked rosy-red on a blush pink to white background. Occasional shoots produce self-red flowers and these may be propagated to produce the form 'Contessa Lavinia Maggi Rosea'. It is advisable to remove branches with self-red flowers since almost complete reversion has been observed on some old specimens. This is one of the best double striped camellias and opens most of its flowers in one flush. 'Contessa Lavinia Maggi' was raised in Italy about 1850.

'Contessa Lavinia Maggi Rosea' was first exhibited in 1867 by William Bull, which indicates that this self-red sport

92

Plate 8. 'Hornsby Pink' at Tregothnan, Cornwall. The formal, double flowers of this *C. japonica* cultivar are of ranunculus form and resemble those of 'Myrtifolia'

Plate 9. 'Elegans'. This hardy and free-flowering cultivar of *C. japonica* produces large, anemone-form flowers on young plants and peony-form flowers on older specimens

Plate 10. *C. x williamsii* 'J. C. WILLIAMS'. This famous Cornish *williamsii* hybrid was named after its originator at Caerhays. It has the longest flower period and is remarkably hardy and prolific

Plate 11. *C. x williamsii* 'GEORGE BLANDFORD'. A Caerhays hybrid from *C. saluenensis x C. japonica* 'Elegans'

occurred at an early date. One wonders if it could have been the original form of the variety since it will sometimes dominate the bush if left unchecked.

'DONCKELARII'. A very slow-growing pendulous bush with small, narrow, glossy, dark green leaves on slender drooping branches. The semi-double crimson flowers are often attractively marbled white, though there is a self-red form named 'Eugene Bolen'. The loose rounded petals are produced in two conical, overlapping layers, the lower flowers hanging pendulous by their own weight, in which position they are considerably protected from adverse weather. Late flowering. There are several branch sports of 'Donckelarii', including 'Ville de Nantes', darker red, blotched white with frilled, erect petals: similar is 'Donckelarii Frisée'.

'Donckelarii' was introduced from Japan along with 'Tricolor' by Franz von Siebold in 1829. It is recorded that Dr Siebold's importation, which included a considerable collection of oriental plants, was unloaded at Antwerp in 1831, whilst the French were beseiging the citadel. The cases in which they were packed became badly damaged on the quay-side during the transhipment of a cavalry contingent and the remnants were passed on to the expert care of one André Donckelaar, chief gardener of the University of Louvain, and later of the Ghent Botanical Gardens, and subsequently named after him. Both the varieties mentioned have similar characteristics, and one cannot help wondering if they were raised by the same nurseryman in Japan.

'ELEGANS' (Chandleri 'Elegans'). This is one of the most popular of the old cultivars, forming a spreading bush with distinctive foliage. On young plants the rose-pink flowers are very large and anemone form with two outer rows of large, flat petals around a central boss of twisted pink petaloids. The flowers on older bushes are a little smaller and exclusively of peony-form shape, the petaloids becoming

93

further modified into petals. Named branch sports include
'C. M. Wilson', light pink, and 'Shiro Chan', pure white.
The flowers of 'Elegans' and its mutants are very weather-
resistant. (Plate 9.)

'Elegans' was raised by Alfred Chandler of Vauxhall in
1819 as a recorded cross between 'Anemonaeflora' and 'Variegata' (the old 'Double Striped' camellia). It is still widely
grown and listed by most camellia growers and is popular
as a Christmas-flowering pot plant in France, Belgium and
Holland, always budding well as a young plant when grown
under glass. Whilst the original 'Elegans' was self-pink there
are forms which bear flowers with white markings. In America the self-pink form is generally known as 'Francine'.

'FRAU MINNA SEIDEL' ('Pink Perfection'). Another vigorous,
erect grower, bearing small, formal double, shell-pink flowers over a considerable period. A branch sport named 'Pink
Pearl' has high, pointed, ivory-centred flowers.

Known in Japan as 'Usu-Otome', this camellia was imported into Germany in 1893 by T. J. Seidel, a nurseryman
of Dresden, and renamed after his wife. The name 'Otome'
is applied by the Japanese to a group of camellias with small
imbricated flowers. The leaves are paler than those of most
camellias. The plants flower freely, often shedding some of
their overcrowded buds as they commence to swell. The
blossoms last well when cut, gradually fading to white.

'GLOIRE DE NANTES'. A compact bushy grower with bold, lustrous dark green foliage. It is the earliest coloured cultivar
of C. japonica in general circulation, bearing large, semi-
double rose-pink flowers in prolonged succession often from
January to April. It usually sheds any frost-damaged flowers
and is worthy of a favoured situation on account of its long
flower period. The American cultivar 'Lady Ruth' is a rose-
pink and white branch sport of 'Gloire de Nantes'.

'HAKU-RAKUTEN' ('Wisley White') is probably the most satisfactory white variety for outdoor cultivation. The large, semi-double to peony-form flowers have curved and fluted petals which are remarkably weatherproof. It forms a vigorous, erect bush, flowering mid-season to late.

'IMBRICATA RUBRA'. A vigorous, erect variety with bold, attractively twisted and well-spaced leaves which sometimes display a creamy yellow mottling and variegation much sought after as a cut foliage. The medium-large formal double, light red, imbricated flowers are borne almost entirely on the tips of long slender shoots. These, too, provide excellent cut material, lasting well if picked in the coloured bud stage. The one-year shoots are an attractive golden brown turning to silvery grey bark on older branches. It makes an excellent hedge plant on account of its slender, erect growth.

'Imbricata Rubra' was brought back from China by John Damper Parks in 1824 and originally christened 'Imbricata', the name 'Rubra' being added later to distinguish it from 'Imbricata Alba'.

'LADY CLARE'. This variety has already been cited as one of the most spreading and prostrate of the Japonicas. The large, semi-double rose-pink flowers open flat along the upper side of the horizontal to prostrate branches. The leaves are large and sharply toothed and pointed, with raised venation.

'Lady Clare' is probably the Japanese variety 'Akashi-gata', and was originally introduced into Belgium about 1887, after which it achieved a wide distribution.

'LATIFOLIA' has flowers resembling those of 'Lady Clare' but the growth habit is more bushy and the leaves are exceptionally large and broad with rounded teeth and raised venation. The branch sport 'Nagasaki' ('Lady Audrey Buller') has similar flowers marbled white in varying degrees. It is said to be a triploid.

'MAGNOLIAEFLORA' is the old Japanese variety 'Hagoromo',

95

which was introduced into Italy in 1886. It has the neat, tight foliage and growth of 'Tricolor' with medium, semi-double, blush-pink flowers, the long and narrow petals being arranged in two layers. The flowers bear a resemblance to those of *Magnolia stellata*. The white form of 'Magnoliaeflora Alba' is the Japanese 'Yobeki-Dori' and is flushed pink. These are very slow-growing types and are sometimes more costly, size for size, than most other *C. japonica* cultivars.

'MATHOTIANA' ('Purple Emperor'). A very large rose form to formal double crimson, sometimes showing a remarkable purple cast on the old blooms. The growth is compact with bright green, glossy, slender-pointed foliage. This variety is sometimes known as 'Mathotiana Rubra'. It is not related vegetatively to other 'Mathotiana' varieties.

'MATHOTIANA ALBA'. Large formal double white, late flowering. The branches of mature plants are almost horizontal and they show a remarkable disinclination to produce side branches so that terminal shoots continue to grow slowly outwards from the centre of the bush. The foliage is light green to yellow in hot sunny situations. The leaves are broadly rounded, of a very leathery texture. Branch sports include 'Mathotiana Rosea', clear pink, and 'Souv. de Bahuaud Litou', with large blush-pink flowers. 'Mathotiana Alba' and its branch sports flower late, the blossoms opening flat and then reflexing when mature.

'MIKADO'. An unusual bicolor variety bearing large, semi-double dark red flowers margined white. Medium- to late-flowering. A similar variety, 'The Mikado' is a sport of 'Herme' and has rose-pink flowers with white-edged petals and narrow twisted leaves. These are mutants or branch sports of the old Japanese variety 'Hikaru-Genji'. The similar names have caused some confusion.

'MONSTRUOSO RUBRA' ('Gigantea'). A very large red, semi-double, anemone-form to peony-form, of vigorous open growth. The leaves are almost orbicular, stiff and leathery, margined with small, sharp teeth. This variety is a triploid.

'NOBILISSIMA'. Much has been written already in praise of this double white variety which has the longest flowering period of all white camellias. The leaves are light green with raised venation and the growth habit is erect and vigorous. The mature blossoms sometimes display a creamy-yellow cast, and are peony-form, sometimes displaying mixed petals and petaloids. There is a scarce pink form named 'Nobilissima Rosea'.

'OPTIMA'. This variety has been already mentioned on account of its remarkably stiff, erect habit which makes it suitable for planting in confined spaces. The manner in which the blush-pink, crimson-streaked flowers are borne close to the erect shoots, as though fastened artificially, has been mentioned too. The foliage is broad and light green with waved, sharply-toothed margins. The branch sport 'Wally Abbiss' is a self-pink cultivar named by me.

'RUBESCENS MAJOR'. This outstanding cultivar makes a compact bush, the stout, leathery leaves showing conspicuously raised veins. The large, formal, double flowers are a bright rosy red colour with crimson veins and display tight rose-bud centres when they commence to open. A very tough and reliable variety which appears to have been introduced from France about 1910, but its precise origin is unknown.

'TRICOLOR' (Siebold). This is the best-known of three different camellias which bear the name 'Tricolor'. It forms a compact, erect bush, the short, stiff shoots being closely clad with narrow, sharply pointed and slightly twisted leaves. The large semi-double flowers are blush-pink to white with bold, radial, carmine-red streaks down the centres of the distinctively cupped, waxy textured petals. The blossoms are borne tightly along the branches at the ends of short side shoots and are remarkably weatherproof. Occasional shoots may bear self-red or partly self-red blossoms in the same manner as that already described for 'Contessa Lavinia Maggi'.

'Tricolor' (Siebold) was introduced into Belgium together with 'Donckelarii' by Dr Siebold in 1829 and was rescued from a cavalry affray on the quayside at Antwerp as described under 'Donckelarii'. 'Tricolor' is a very old variety which has given rise to numerous variants from branch sports. These include the self-coloured forms 'Lady de Saumarez' ('Tricolor Red'), 'Tricolor Pink' and 'Leucantha' ('Tricolor White'). 'Lady Mackinnon' is carmine, marbled white, whilst 'Tricolor Folki' is red with white blotches. The American variety 'Lady de Saumarez' is not a self-red but has white stripes and may well have sported thus after its introduction from Jersey, where it originated. 'Fred Sander' ('Fimbriata Superba') is a self-crimson with frilled petals closely resembling those of the 'Donckelarii' branch sport 'Ville de Nantes', adding yet another similarity to these two camellias which arrived in Europe on the same ship almost 140 years ago. 'Tricolor' is a very unstable plant liable to produce both single and semi-double flowers and often producing several of the above colour variants on the same bush.

'WHITE SWAN'. A rounded bush bearing large, funnel-shaped, white flowers with conspicuous golden stamens. Early to mid-season. Best in shade and shelter. 'Amabilis' ('Yukumi-Guruma') has single white flowers which open flat and is sometimes incorrectly referred to as 'Alba Simplex'. It has splayed stamens, characteristic of the Higo group of camellias, many of which have a tendency to turn black soon after the flowers open.

AMERICAN VARIETIES OF CAMELLIA JAPONICA

Because *Camellia japonica* seldom bears fertile seed in

English gardens, comparatively few new varieties have been raised here until quite recently. Apparently camellia pollen requires a higher temperature for germination than that usually obtaining out of doors during the spring. In many parts of America, however, the climate appears to be ideal in this respect and countless new varieties have been raised and named, especially during the last fifteen years.

The following is a selection from more recent American introductions which have shown promise in British gardens.

'AUBURN WHITE'. Probably the latest *C. japonica* cultivar, often at its best in early June. The very large semi-double flowers open flat and gradually fade from blush pink to white so that the name is almost self-descriptive. The colour is identical to that of 'Mrs D. W. Davis', but the buds are not overcrowded and the flowers open wider and much later.

'BEAU HARP'. Very erect and compact with large, blood-red, peony-form flowers. Early to mid-season.

'CLAUDIA PHELPS'. Delicate pink edged and sometimes splashed with white.

'C. M. WILSON'. Light pink sport of 'Elegans' with large, anemone-form flowers. Early to mid-season, of slow, spreading habit.

'DEBUTANTE' ('Sara C. Hastie'). Medium-large, light pink, peony-form; vigorous erect growth. Early to mid-season.

'DRAMA GIRL'. Very large, semi-double, deep salmon rose-pink. Forms an open, spreading bush with pendulous branches.

'ELEANOR HAGOOD'. Formal double pale pink, opening late. Growth vigorous and erect.

'GUILIO NUCCIO'. A vigorous, erect bush with long, tapering 'Arejishi'-type foliage. The large, semi-double, coral pink flowers have velvety textured petals. Mid-season.

'HIGH HAT'. Light pink sport of 'Daikagura' with deeper venation. Large peony-form flowers opening early. Slow, compact growth.

'J. J. WHITFIELD'. A vigorous, erect grower with long, saw-edged leaves and darkest red peony-form flowers born all along the shoots. Early to mid-season.

'JOSEPH PFINGSTL'. A compact, erect bush with attractive, glossy foliage. The large, dark red flowers are semi-double to peony-form. Early to mid-season.

'LETITIA SCHRADER'. An erect, compact bush with intense, crimson scarlet, peony-form to anemone-form flowers. Mid-season.

'MADGE MILLER'. ('Chandleri Alba'). A rounded bush with slender, glossy foliage and remarkably weatherproof, white, anemone-form flowers. Mid-season.

'MARJORIE MAGNIFICENT'. A very vigorous and compact grower with semi-double to anemone-form, light pink flowers. Early to mid-season.

'MRS D. W. DAVIS'. In English gardens it forms an open, spreading bush with bold, glossy leaves, but in America it is described as being erect and compact. The flowers are blush-pink, very large and semi-double, remaining cup-shaped for some time before opening fully.

'MONTE CARLO'. A light pink sport of 'Finlandia', producing large, semi-double flowers with swirled and fluted petals. Compact habit.

'R. L. WHEELER'. A vigorous, erect grower, its broad, matt-surfaced leaves are puckered and recurved along the margins. The flower buds are coated with loose scale-like sepals and open to very large, rose-pink, semi-double to anemone-form flowers with broad outer petals and a central boss of petaloids and stamens. Early to mid-season.

'SIERRA SPRING'. Variegated form of the variety 'Mme Hahn'. A bright pink and white semi-double of vigorous, erect growth.

'TOMORROW'. Large strawberry-red, semi-double varying to peony-form. Vigorous open habit. Early to mid-season.

'WHITE GIANT'. A large semi-double with flowers very weatherproof for a white variety. Growth vigorous, compact and erect.

'YOURS TRULY'. Sport of 'Lady Vansittart'. Medium, semi-double flowers, the broad, wavy edged petals are pink with deeper streaks and edged white. Of slow, bushy growth with narrow twisted leaves. Mid-season to late.

Many other varieties are now on trial in Britain and some of these will no doubt qualify as good garden plants. Some have proved unsuitable either because their flowers are too large to withstand the effect of rain and wind, or because they tend to produce too great a mass of flower buds on the tips of their shoots and so require regular disbudding if good-quality blooms are to be produced.

The 1967-8 Popularity Poll, organized by the American Camellia Society, listed as the ten most popular varieties:

'BETTY SHEFFIELD SUPREME'. Large semi-double to loose peony form, white, with deep pink or red margins to the slightly waved petals, medium compact grower.

'GUILIO NUCCIO'. See previous list.

'VILLE DE NANTES'. A sport of the old variety 'Donckelarii' mentioned earlier in this chapter. A large semi-double with erect, dark red, frilled or fimbriated petals, sometimes blotched white. (Plate 6.)

'TIFFANY'. Very large light orchid pink, deeper at the edges. Loose peony-form to anemone-form, vigorous, upright growth. Mid-season.

101

'CARTER'S SUNBURST'. Large pale pink, semi-double to peony-form to formal double with petals striped or marked deeper pink. Compact grower.

'MATHOTIANA SUPREME'. Sport of 'Mathotiana'. A very large semi-double with loose, irregular petals interspersed with stamens.

'DRAMA GIRL'. See previous list.

'JULIA FRANCE'. Very large light pink, semi-double, with fluted petals. Very large leaves. Mid-season.

'KRAMER'S SUPREME'. Very large Turkey Red peony-form. Vigorous erect grower.

'MRS D. W. DAVIS'. See previous list.

Recent American raisings imported by English Camellia grower David Trehane of Wimborne, Dorset and recommended by him include:

'BERENICE BODDY'. Light pink with deeper reverse, medium semi-double. A vigorous, erect grower with a hardy reputation.

'EMMETT BARNES'. Large white semi-double with ruffled and twisted petals intermixed. Compact-grower.

'GRAND SLAM'. A very large clear red anemone-form with two or three rows of wavy recurving petals. A spreading grower with broad, dark green leaves.

'MISS UNIVERSE'. Large white peony form. Vigorous erect grower.

'REG RAGLAND'. Very large semi-double red with smaller centre petals surrounding a mass of yellow stamens. A compact grower with a prolonged flowering period.

'SPRING SONNET'. Pale pink, deepening towards margins.

'TOMORROW PARK HILL'. A sport of 'Tomorrow' with soft pink semi-double flowers, deeper towards the edges of the petals, with some white variegation.

Mention should be made of the existence of mini-flowered camellias, ranging from the old Japanese cultivar 'Bokuhan', a single dark red with creamy-white petaloids, to the American cultivars 'Tinker Bell' and 'Jingle Bells', the former having very small anemone-form white flowers striped pink and red whilst the latter is a self-red sport of the former.

IX

The Williamsii Hybrids

The history of these hybrids begins with the introduction
by that famous plant collector George Forrest of several
newly discovered wild species of camellia, from Yunnan in
northern China, during various plant-hunting expeditions
which he made to that area between 1910 and 1932; Forrest
was commissioned by the Edinburgh Botanic Gardens and
aided by a syndicate of private subscribers.

CAMELLIA SALUENENSIS

The most important of these Chinese introductions, from
our point of view, arrived under Forrest's number 17686,
and was ultimately named *Camellia saluenensis* (Plate 1),
after its habitat in the Salween River Valley. Typical plants
of *C. saluenensis* have long, narrow, dark green leaves which
usually display a characteristic reticulation, the veins being
conspicuously sunken or impressed, though, at a glance,
they appear to be raised.

The flowers are single, on some plants opening flat, on
others remaining funnel-shaped. The colour is very rarely
white, occasionally pale pink and more often rose-pink. The
ovaries, which become conspicuous after the flowers fall
away, are coated with silky hairs, whilst those of *C. japonica*
are bald. Most seedlings commence to flower in their third
or fourth year, whereas those of *C. japonica* may take ten
years or more. I have known seedlings of *C. saluenensis* to

blossom when only one year old, but this is exceptional. This newly introduced species also turned out to be a prolific seed-bearer, whereas *C. japonica* does not often set fertile seed in English gardens, except for some very old plants of the single flowered forms. Most camellia apples on *C. japonica* in this climate are parthenocarpic, or abortive, since they do not contain fertile seeds.

These qualities make *C. saluenensis* an ideal female or seed parent for breeding from if blooms are emasculated by removing the stamens before they ripen and the stigmas inoculated with pollen selected from another camellia chosen as the male parent.

At Borde Hill in Sussex, there is a tall isolated specimen of *C. saluenensis* growing close to the north park fence facing across open countryside with no protection whatever. It continues to flower profusely over a long period and is remarkably weatherproof.

There is evidence that a considerable amount of variation and even hybridity was present in the original seedlings raised as *C. saluenensis* in such gardens as Caerhays and the identity of some of the other species introduced by Forrest, such as *C. pitardii* in its different geographical forms, seems to have been lost sight of. In his *Revision of the Genus CAMELLIA* (1958), J. Robert Sealy wrote:

'For centuries Yunnan has been famous for the cultivation of camellias—what effect this long tradition of camellia cultivation may have had on the present distribution of the plants, we do not know, but obviously it is a point to be borne in mind when considering distribution of the plants in Yunnan.'

There are several named cultivars of *C. saluenensis* including:

'Bartley Pink'. Small, single, bright pink flowers and narrow waxy leaves.

'Bow Bells'. Rose-pink and funnel-shaped with darker veins.

105

Mid-season to late. (Some authorities list this as a *C. x 'williamsii'*.)

'Exbury Trumpet'. An early, single, phlox pink with large funnel-shaped blossoms. (Plate 1.)

'Merryn Galsworthy'. The largest flowered *C. saluenensis* we have yet come across, with extra-fine light pink flowers opening flat, mid-season to late.

CAMELLIA x WILLIAMSII

The late John Charles Williams of Caerhays Castle, Cornwall, was a member of the syndicate which supported Forrest's expeditions. In the shelter of his extensive woodland garden, close to the shore of Veryan Bay, he raised and planted many of Forrest's introductions. Using selected plants of *Camellia saluenensis* as female parents he made a series of crosses, using pollen from plants of *C. japonica* and showing a marked preference for the single-flowered forms.

The resulting hybrids, now know universally as *Camellia x williamsii*, included such well-known varieties as 'J. C. Williams', single light pink, and 'St Ewe', phlox pink. A later series of crosses using 'Lady Clare' as the male parent gave rise to those remarkable fully double varieties 'Caerhays' and 'George Blandford', the latter flowering very early, both being of a bright rosy-red, the former with a pronounced purple cast.

Other plant enthusiasts followed in his footsteps, but these and all future hybrids between *C. japonica* and *C. saluenensis* will be forever known as *Camellia x williamsii*, in honour of the famous Cornish plantsman in whose hands the first crosses were made.

Another outstanding hybrid which he raised is *Camellia x 'Cornish Snow'*, made, as previously mentioned, by crossing *C. saluenensis* with *C. cuspidata*, a close relative of the Chinese Tea Plant. This cultivar bears a long succession of small single white flowers opening from carmine-tinted buds. The original form had pale yellow stamens, but a reverse cross made later has bright golden stamens, which, in our opinion, improves the appearance of the flowers, and which often commence to open in February and continue into April.

The foliage of *Camellia* x 'Cornish Snow' is narrow and pointed, and much daintier than that of most other camellias. In summer the young leaves are stained a deep purple, gradually shading to green as the growth ripens. In the former state the foliage makes magnificent material for floral arrangement for those fortunate enough to have plants sufficiently large for cutting from.

Best known of the 'Williamsii' hybrids which have originated to date beyond the confines of Caerhays is *C.* x *williamsii* 'Donation', a cross between *C. saluenensis* and *C. japonica* 'Donckelarii' made in the Sussex garden of Borde Hill, by Walter Fleming, head gardener to the late Colonel Stephenson Clarke. It is one of the most prolific flowerers, a semi-double of a delicate silvery pink with deeper veins and of vigorous, erect growth. It received an Award of Merit from the Royal Horticultural Society in 1941 but was probably bred as early as 1928. (Plate 12.)

In another famous Cornish garden at Trewithen, a seedling of *Camellia* x *williamsii* 'Donation' from natural fertilization has produced that remarkable variety 'Glenn's Orbit', named to commemorate the American astronaut's space flight. It has even larger flowers than 'Donation', without the deeper coloured veins, and commences to bloom a month to six weeks earlier. It has usually almost finished flowering by the time that the first flowers on 'Donation' commence to open. (Plate 13.)

The 'Williamsii' hybrids exhibit a hybrid vigour in their prolific flower-bud development which is usually more profuse than that of most of the older *japonica* varieties. They

107

have developed a reputation for flowering freely in northern latitudes where *Camellia japonica* cultivars are shy of flowering.

The severe winter in Britain of 1962–3 completely defoliated most of the large original bushes of *C. saluenensis* at Caerhays but they completely recovered during the two following growth seasons. The 'Williamsii' hybrids fared much better and even flowered normally, though late, after the severe cold had departed. The *japonicas*, though their foliage generally was unaffected by the cold, produced flowers which were much below normal size.

The reason why the 'Williamsii' hybrids flower normally after severe winters may be due to the fact that they commence bud initiation at least a month earlier than *C. japonica*, so that their flower crop is already assured by late autumn when the buds of most *C. japonica* cultivars are only commencing to develop.

Perhaps the most important feature about the 'Williamsii' hybrids from a garden point of view is that they are self-grooming, for they immediately shed spent and weather-damaged flowers instead of retaining them as an eyesore in the manner of many cultivars of *C. japonica*.

There is no doubt whatever that the 'Williamsii' hybrids have done more than anything else to popularize camellias as garden plants since they flower freely in colder climates than suits the cultivars of *C. japonica*. They have also proved to be hardier than *C. japonica*, which is rather surprising since *C. saluenensis* is generally regarded as being rather less so. What remarkable improvements have been achieved in so short a period.

Most of the 'Williamsii' hybrids commence to bloom several weeks before the majority of the Japonica cultivars. At Caerhays the peak period for their hybrids is about mid-March whilst the Japonicas are not usually at their best until mid-April. 1963 was an exception, when camellias of

Plate 12. *C. x williamsii* 'DONA-TION'. This semi-double Sussex-raised hybrid of *C. saluenensis* x *C. japonica* 'Donckelarii' has become the most popular camellia in the world

Plate 13. *C. x williamsii* 'GLENN'S ORBIT', which resulted from an isolated and possibly apomictic seed of *C. x williamsii* 'Donation', which occurred at Trewithen in Cornwall

Plate 14. C. x 'SALUTATION'. The original seedling of this controversial hybrid between *C. saluenensis* and *C. reticulata* 'Captain Rawes' at Borde Hill, Sussex. March 1967

Plate 15. C. x 'INSPIRATION'. This semi-double hybrid was bred from *C. reticulata simplex* and *C. saluenensis*

all kinds flowered together about ten days after the prolonged frosts. The flowers of the 'Williamsii' hybrids were as good as ever but there was a marked reduction in size and quality among the Japonicas.

An air frost of 14°F on the last night of March 1967 devastated all opening buds on our rhododendrons and evergreen azaleas and seared the young shoots on most evergreen and many deciduous trees and shrubs. Most of our camellias were in full flower and it was interesting to observe that white flowers were affected most whilst dark red ones, 'Nigra' ('Kouron Jura'), in particular were scarcely harmed at all. The fully open flowers on a plant of 'Arejishi' also escaped unmarked. Among the paler shades, the flowers of *C. saluenensis* and the 'Williamsii' hybrids suffered only slightly, and, being self-grooming, they were soon looking immaculate again. Recent research has revealed that red flowers absorb heat more readily than white ones, their temperature being as much as 15°F warmer.

FRAGRANCE IN CAMELLIA x WILLIAMSII HYBRIDS

During a visit to Caerhays one February afternoon I was surprised at the subtle fragrance emitted by some of the 'Williamsii' hybrids. The air was very still, the sky completely overcast, and the temperature low. The previous day had been bright and abnormally warm for the time of year.

Among the single cultivars, 'Mary Jobson' seemed unique in this respect. The mother plant, which is growing on the north face of the castle, was in full bloom and filled the forecourt with a pleasing but elusive perfume, the source of which had not been established before. It would be interesting to know if similar reports are available from other gardens.

109

A SELECTION OF *CAMELLIA x WILLIAMSII* CULTIVARS

'Beatrice Michael'. Single blush-pink, mid-season to late and very prolific. Colour similar to 'Charles Michael' but opening flatter in one sensational display. Dark and glossy foliage with impressed reticulate venation.

'Caerhays'. (*C. saluenensis* x *C. japonica* 'Lady Clare'.) This hybrid displays a most distinctive trait, the leaves being abnormally long and tapering, very glossy and often with a peculiar rippled and puckered surface. The main shoot is usually erect with almost horizontal side branches, a tendency which makes this camellia ideal for training against a wall. The bright ruby-red flowers are large and fully double, varying from anemone-form to peony-form and sometimes displaying a pronounced purple cast. This hybrid generally flowers four to six weeks later than its brother variety 'George Blandford'.

'Carolyn Williams'. An unusual bicolor which arose as a self-sown seedling at Caerhays, with large flat flowers carried almost entirely face downwards, the broad pink petals being boldly streaked with carmine.

'Charles Michael'. A late blush-pink with long-petalled, trumpet-shaped flowers. Foliage with reticulate venation like *C. saluenensis*.

'Citation'. Large, semi-double, pale silvery pink with irregular petals. Vigorous, open erect growth and long narrow leaves. Declared a 'Williamsii' hybrid by the raiser but considered a *reticulata* hybrid by the author (see page 128).

'Donation' (*C. saluenensis* x *C. japonica* 'Donckelarii'). Large, semi-double, silvery pink with darker veins. Compact, erect habit. Very free flowering, mid-season. Leaves small and glossy, vigorous grower. Truly a most outstanding garden plant, worthy of the highest praise. There appears to be more than one form of this hybrid; see notes at the end of this chapter. (Plate 12.)

'Elizabeth de Rothschild' (*C. saluenensis* x *C. japonica* 'Adolphe Audusson'). Semi-double rose-pink. Mid-season to late. Foliage resembles *C. saluenensis*.

'Francis Hanger' (*C. saluenensis* x *C. japonica* 'Alba Simplex'). Single white and flowering with such freedom that the branches become weighed down with flower buds, a tendency which weakens the bush. The foliage is broad and tends towards *C. japonica*.

'George Blandford' (*C. saluenensis* x *C. japonica* 'Lady Clare'). Brother to 'Caerhays', it is from four to six weeks earlier. Bears large, fully double, rosy-red, anemone- to peony-form flowers. Of low spreading habit and very difficult to propagate. Leaves have reticulated, impressed venation. Both varieties are quite outstanding. (Plate 11.)

'Glenn's Orbit'. Daughter of 'Donation' from a natural fertilization, this outstanding seedling produces larger and paler pink flowers up to two months before those of the parent commence to open. These are semi-double and have broader petals without the deeper veining characteristic of 'Donation'. Foliage tougher and broader than 'Donation's'. It flowers about the same time as 'George Blandford'. (Plate 13.)

'Golden Spangles'. A variegated-leaved form of 'Mary Christian' with leaf centres flushed gold. Flowers phlox-pink, single. *C. saluenensis* type foliage. It originated somewhat mysteriously at the R.H.S. Garden at Wisley from a plant of 'Mary Christian' supplied from Caerhays which apparently sported.

'Hiraethlyn'. A vigorous, erect grower with large, single, orchid-pink, funnel-shaped blossoms. The foliage is narrow and lustreless, tending towards *C. saluenensis*. Raised at Bodnant in North Wales.

'J. C. Williams'. Raised by and named to commemorate the originator of these hybrids, this well-known cultivar bears an abnormally long succession of single, blush-pink blossoms which open flat along almost horizontal branches,

111

clad with slightly undulating, lustreless foliage. Has a longer flower period than any other 'Williamsii' camellia in our collection. Unfortunately often confused with 'Philippa Forwood'. (Plate 10.)

'John Pickthorn'. An erect, late-flowering hybrid with single, deep pink trumpets and narrow, glossy foliage.

'Mary Christian'. Single phlox-pink. Open erect habit, dainty, polished foliage tending towards *C. japonica*.

'Mary Jobson'. Early to mid-season. Light pink with single flowers opening flat and broad smooth leaves like *C. japonica*.

'Mary Larcom'. A spreading bush with large, light pink flowers which open flat. One of the latest to commence to flower and continuing for a considerable period. The flowers are remarkably fragrant under certain weather conditions.

'Mildred Veitch'. (*C. saluenensis* x *C. japonica* 'Elegans'). A large, semi-double to anemone-form, with orchid-pink petals. The growth is slow, compact and erect and the foliage is small, resembling *C. saluenensis* rather than *C. japonica*. Raised on the Exeter nurseries of Messrs Robert Veitch & Sons.

'November Pink'. This name was suggested by the writer when he first saw this unusually early hybrid flowering in a sheltered corner in the woodland garden at Caerhays in November 1950. Its adoption by the late Mr Charles Williams, when he exhibited the plant at an R.H.S. Show a fortnight later, came as a pleasant surprise. This hybrid has small, glossy, *saluenensis*-type foliage on long, redenned stems producing very few side shoots, and bears large, single, phlox-pink flowers opening flat over a long period from autumn to early spring. Sensationally early.

'Philippa Forwood'. Single blush-pink. A vigorous, erect grower, often confused with 'J. C. Williams'.

'Rosemary Williams'. Single, bright rose-pink. Very prolific. Flower colour similar to 'St Ewe' but opening flat in one flush. Growth compact and erect, with attractive, glossy foliage.

112

'St Ewe'. Large, single, rose-pink, funnel-shaped flowers commencing early and continuing to open over a long period. Erect, bushy habit with glossy leaves on reddened shoots.

CAMELLIA x WILLIAMSII 'DONATION'
Clone or Grex?

(*Clone* is the term applied to all plants propagated vegetatively, either directly or indirectly from one original plant. *Grex* is the term applied to a group of crosses or hybrids of the same parentage.)

' "Donation" is perhaps the most vigorous of the Williamsii hybrids.' So wrote Mr Julian Williams in a letter to me, praising with his customary modesty a plant raised by someone else in preference to any of the wide range of Camellias which had originated at Caerhays.

The 'Donation' we had been propagating was definitely not very vigorous; in fact, it was quite the slowest of them, forming an open-branched bush with no sign of the sturdy, erect shoots generally associated with this Camellia. The flowers seemed to have broader petals without the fluted shaping characteristics of those of the erect-growing form. Surely then there must be more than one clone of 'Donation'.

Several experienced Camellia growers have agreed with my contention, among them Mr John Russell of Windlesham (who has since wavered somewhat, although it was he who started the hare), without any prompting from me during a lunch party at which we were both guests at Borde Hill in March 1967. Accompanied by Lady Clarke, we made a careful examination of the older plants of 'Donation' and found one which had only just commenced to open a solitary flower at the very top of the bush, whilst all of the others were already in full bloom. Although we made careful comparisons of flowers from different plants, apart from this one, we came away without arriving at any definite conclusion.

Brian Doe, head gardener at Borde Hill at that time, wrote: 'As you are, I am of the opinion there must have been other seedlings from the same pod as Camellia "Dona-tion". I raised the question with Walter Fleming who was Colonel Clarke's head gardener and who actually made the cross, and it appeared there were several *saluenensis* x *japon-ica* "Donckelarii" crosses made and the resulting seed sown as one batch. They were grown on for proving in Gore's Wood, which was where "Donation" turned up. The *saluenensis* used as seed parent was the pale apple blossom coloured form that flowers six to eight weeks earlier than the type.'

Mr Jim Moffatt, head gardener to Major Norman Colville at Penheale Manor near Launceston, Cornwall, also readily agreed with me immediately after I made mention of my theory. He promptly took me out to the woodland garden and showed me the two forms, with yet a third of deeper colour which he has kept under observation for several seasons. He also showed me several seedlings which he had raised, many of which were flowering for the first time at ten years of age. Amongst them was one very like 'Donation' which he had bred by crossing *C. saluenensis* with *C. japon-ica* 'Adolphe Audusson'. In a similar cross Miss Carlyon of Tregrehan has raised two almost identical 'Donation'-like seedlings one of which she has named 'Edward Carlyon'.

Mr S. A. Pearce, late Deputy Curator at the Royal Botanic Gardens, Kew, also readily agreed with my contention and later wrote: 'I quite agree that the name "Donation" should be treated as a grex in the same way as we adopt for Rhodo-dendron hybrids, because there are without question a num-ber of forms of this camellia in cultivation. I have in mind the very excellent form which has been grown at Wakehurst Place for years and also one can find quite a number of plants of "Donation" in other gardens which do vary not only in colour but in form of flower, and this is borne out very strongly when one views exhibits at the Camellia exhibition at R.H.S. Shows.

'One must allow of course for local conditions, seasons

and the weather, which we know full well does upset the flowering of many Camellias from time to time, but generally speaking "Donation" of all the *williamsii* hybrids does hold pride of place in gardens and therefore your investigation into the possibilities of the forms which may exist is very essential. The large plants of "Donation" at Wisley are another example of a particularly good form, and also Mr. Puddle at Bodnant has a form which is always to me exceptionally good so far as colour is concerned.'

Let me cite here other definite instances of very similar seedlings which have resulted from recorded crosses. The double *williamsii* hybrids 'Caerhays' and 'George Blandford', resulting from *C. saluenensis* x *C. japonica* 'Lady Clare', bear flowers which, at certain periods, are so similar as to be scarcely distinguishable. They are, however, different in growth habit, and 'George Blandford' usually commences to bloom several weeks before 'Caerhays'. These same differences are apparent in the two assumed forms of 'Donation'.

A careful look into the results of controlled crosses made in America, Australia and New Zealand reveals many similar twins, triplets and even quads resulting from the same parents, even when a cross is repeated in reverse. In England the two Caerhays clones of 'Cornish Snow', achieved thus, are only distinguishable to the casual observer by the colour of their stamens, sulphur yellow in the original and bright gold in the reverse cross.

When 'Donation' was raised at Borde Hill way back about 1927 it is unlikely that the original cross should have produced only one fertile seed, especially bearing in mind that the female parent was *C. saluenensis*. Walter Fleming, who actually made the cross, stated that he repeated it on many flowers of *C. saluenensis* using pollen from *C. japonica* 'Donckelarii' and that he raised a considerable number of seedlings. Were they subsequently distributed as *C.* x 'Donation' in the manner in which hybrid rhododendrons have

115

been named and distributed in the past, so that clonal names have had to be added to distinguished cultivars within the grex of group of hybrids? I suggest that this is the most likely explanation and clearly the problem requires fuller investigation which would take considerable time. Indeed it may never be finally resolved through lack of original detail in the Borde Hill records and the fact that 'Donation' in its one or several clones is now distributed throughout the world wherever camellias can be grown. I wonder if any other camellia breeder has repeated this cross and, if so, did his or her seedlings resemble 'Donation' and what proportion of them produced semi-double flowers.

SOME AMERICAN AND AUSTRALIAN CULTIVARS OF C. x 'WILLIAMSII'

'Bowen Bryant' (Australia). A strong, erect grower bearing large, semi-double, bell-shaped flowers of a clear, silvery pink.

'Brigadoon' (America). (*C. saluenensis* x *C. japonica* 'Princesse Baciocchi'). A compact, erect grower with large, semi-double rose-pink flowers, not unlike 'Donation'.

'E. G. Waterhouse' (Australia). A tall, compact grower with formal double flowers of a soft, silvery pink.

'Felice Harris' (America). A strong, compact grower, the large semi-double orchid-pink flowers having fluted petals.

'Lady Gowrie' (Australia). Has medium, semi-double flowers with notched petals coloured dog-rose pink.

'Margaret Waterhouse' (Australia). A vigorous, erect bush with medium, semi-double, light pink flowers.

'Shocking Pink' (Australia). An upright grower with medium, formal double to peony-form, rose-pink flowers.

'Waltz Time' (America). A bushy grower bearing large, semi-double, lilac-pink flowers.

Already there are several second-generation hybrids made

116

by recrossing varieties of *C.* x *williamsii* with selected cultivars of *C. japonica.* Among them are 'Blue Danube', a strong, upright grower bearing medium to large peony-form flowers of a rosy-lavender colour.

David Trehane, Camellia-grower of Wimborne, Dorset, has been responsible for importing and introducing into English gardens many of the best of recent raisings from America, Australia and New Zealand. He considers that the following varieties are among the best which he grows.

'Anticipation' (New Zealand). A Les Jury hybrid bred from the Australian *C. japonica* 'Leviathan'. A magnificent glowing crimson with peony-form flowers.

'Clarrie Fawcett' (America). Large semi-double rose pink. Erect grower.

'Debbie' (New Zealand). Bred by Les Jury from 'Debutante' with deep pink peony-form flowers.

'Elegant Beauty' (New Zealand). Another Jury hybrid, bred from 'Elegans', with large rosy red, semi-double to peony-form flowers.

'Ellamine' (Australia). Large single pink.

'Elsie Jury' (New Zealand). An exquisite Jury hybrid with clear pink anemone-form flowers with large, deeply cleft outer petals. Of vigorous, erect growth.

'Sayonara' (Australia). Semi-double to rose-form double, clear pink with paler shading towards centre.

117

X

The Reticulata Complex

In 1820 Captain Richard Rawes of the East India Company brought to England a new and distinct camellia from Canton and presented it to his friend Thomas Carey Palmer of Bromley, Kent, in whose conservatory it first flowered in 1826. Although the growth habit was sparse and lanky and the plant somewhat unthrifty, it produced sensationally large, semi-double, rosy crimson flowers some 6 inches across, with attractively waved and fluted petals. It became known as Captain Rawes' Camellia, and was subsequently named *Camellia reticulata* by Lindley because of the pronounced net-like venation impressed into the upper surfaces of its leaves. (Plate 3.)

There can be no doubt that this new introduction caused quite a stir among horticulturists at the time, but unfortunately it proved extraordinarily difficult to propagate. The few cuttings which rooted almost invariably failed to make subsequent growth, so it had to be propagated by grafting, usually by the approach method, onto *Camellia japonica*. Because of its dearth of side shoots and reluctance to respond to pruning, attempts at propagation must have been extremely limited at the outset.

A second introduction was made by John Damper Parks, who went to China for the Royal Horticultural Society in 1823, returning the following year and bringing with him a number of new introductions including *C. japonica* 'Imbricata Rubra'. For the next hundred years Captain Rawes'

118

Camellia was considered to represent the type plant of the species and its perpetuation in Western gardens was assured. Many veterans of this fine camellia flourish against walls, and even in the open, in old mansion gardens in Cornwall. At Caerhays, Tregothnan and Antony House there are bushes of almost tree-like dimensions growing in the open without protection, which vie with the *Arboreum* rhododendrons.

At the Truro Spring Flower Show a special class for the largest specimen bloom is hotly contended by the owners of many famous Cornish gardens. This show is now run by the flourishing Cornwall Garden Society and the long-established status of 'Captain Rawes' (formerly known only as *Camellia reticulata* and then as 'Semi Plena' when the single form appeared) is about to be seriously challenged by other Reticulatas described later in this chapter.

The pollen of *Camellia reticulata* 'Captain Rawes' has proved to be almost completely sterile, so there is little wonder that camellia experts and cytologists have looked upon putative hybrids with suspicion.

In the early 1850s Robert Fortune introduced a second form with fully double flowers, which was named *Camellia reticulata* 'Flore Pleno' in 1857, but is now usually referred to as 'Robert Fortune'. It seems possible that this formal double Reticulata had, in fact, been introduced into England prior to 1850 since there is extant an enthusiastic description of a very large plant only a short time after this date. For some unknown reason this almost disappeared from cultivation during the next hundred years; possibly its introduction was not repeated in the manner that Captain Rawes' variety was, or the difficulties of propagation and desirable distribution were not given the attention which the plant merited. Eventually it joined the ranks of plants presumed lost to cultivation, though it had, in fact, survived in at least two remote camellia collections. (Plate 4.)

119

In the winter of 1951–2, a century after its original introduction into the Western World, it was located again by
famous American camelliophile, the late Mr Ralph Peer,
in the Portuguese nursery of Alfredo Moreira da Silva of
Oporto. How remarkable that this same variety was then
being introduced into America from China as one of the
Kunming Reticulatas under the Chinese name of 'Sungtze-
lin' (literally 'Pine Cone' but now known as 'Pagoda') !
Little wonder that when Dr Yu, in his *Review of Camellia
reticulata and its Garden Varieties* before the Royal Horticultural Society in London in 1950, made no mention of
'Flore Pleno' or 'Robert Fortune'.

A stock of Robert Fortune's Reticulata was also discovered
shortly afterwards in the Caledonia Nurseries, Guernsey, so
its re-introduction was soon under way. Meanwhile, a magnificent specimen flourishing in a Sussex garden had remained unnoticed. It was growing against a wall in Sir Giles
Loder's famous camellia garden at Leonardslee, near Hor-
sham, Sussex, where it is frequently pruned back to the top
of the 16-feet high wall against which it is trained. It originated from the Caledonia Nurseries, Guernsey, early in the
1900s and usually commences to bloom about ten days
earlier than an adjacent specimen of 'Captain Rawes' of
similar age and size.

Apart from being much earlier, the flowers of 'Robert
Fortune' have a remarkable similarity to large, dark red
roses, from the time they commence to open until they are
full-blown, and they are so completely double that there is
seldom any sign of stamens in their centres. It would appear
that Robert Fortune's Reticulata did not reach Cornwall
until about 1955 and, unfortunately, introductions then
from Portugal proved unthrifty until they had become ac-
climatized. It will be many years before any Cornish gardens
can boast a plant as fine as that at Leonardslee.

In China there is reputed to be a fine old specimen 30

feet high with a 20-inch diameter trunk in the grounds of the Capital Hsishan Temple in Kunming. Its planting is believed to date three hundred years back to the building of the temple.

It was not until about 1924 that George Forrest sent home seed of the wild, single forms of *Camellia reticulata,* under his number 25352, which he had discovered as early as 1912 growing on stony hillsides near Tengyueh, in the Chinese province of Yunnan. These plants closely resemble *Camellia saluenensis* apart from being larger in all their parts, developing into big, open-branched shrubs of almost tree-like dimensions. Their leaves are usually leathery and lustreless, with conspicuously impressed venation (reticulation). Their flowers vary from pink to deep rose and are usually funnel-shaped. These are of firm texture, opening and lasting well in water. They fruit freely at Caerhays, where the first seedlings flowered about 1932. The fruits are about the size of clementine oranges with russet casings, which split open to reveal quantities of dark brown seeds, eagerly sought after by mice.

Several selected seedlings have been given clonal names. These include 'Mary Williams' (rosy-crimson) ; 'Trewithen Pink' (rose-pink) and 'Trewithen Salmon', all of which have received the coveted Award of Merit from the Royal Horticultural Society. (Plate 2.)

To distinguish these wild forms of *C. reticulata* from the original introduction by Captain Rawes, they are generally referred to as *Camellia reticulata simplex.* They appear to require more wind protection than *C. saluenensis* on account of their larger leaves and open branching, though *C. reticulata* 'Mary Williams' is more densely furnished and compact. It came through the arctic winter of 1962–3 at Caerhays relatively unscathed when most other forms were completely defoliated and *C. reticulata* 'Captain Rawes' suffered badly in quite a sheltered situation in open woodland. 'Mary Williams' has the added advantage of being relatively easy to root from cuttings and it is the freest flowering form I have seen.

Recognized hybrids between *C. reticulata simplex* and *C. saluenensis* include 'Inamorata' (single rose-pink) and 'Inspiration' (semi-double phlox-pink), whilst 'Leonard Messel' (large semi-double rose-pink) is recorded as having the *williamsii* hybrid 'Mary Christian' as female parent.

Although *Camellia reticulata* 'Captain Rawes' is reputed to be highly sterile, a putative hybrid 'Emperor' was reported to have been raised by a Liverpool horticulturist named Davies as early as the 1840s.

CAMELLIA x 'EMPEROR'

In Verschaffelt's *Nouvelle Iconographie des Camellias,* Tome 111, 1850, Pl. 11, is described and illustrated what was probably the first camellia hybrid raised in the Western world. Though there had already been many new seedlings of *C. japonica* raised and named, some by crossing one variety with pollen from another, none of these were interspecific hybrids.

About ten years earlier a Liverpool horticulturist named Davies had claimed to have crossed a variety of *C. japonica* named 'Colulii' with pollen from *C. reticulata.* The only form of *C. reticulata* available at that date was 'Semi Plena', now known as 'Captain Rawes', whilst the *japonica* cultivar may have been a misprint for 'Colvilii', since this name is on record whilst 'Colulii' is not.

Verschaffelt's colour plate depicts a plant with broad japonica-type foliage and a large red peony-form flower with tightly clustered strap-like petals fading almost to white at the edges. A long-held fallacy that the pollen of *C. reticulata* 'Captain Rawes' was completely sterile, thereby making such a cross impossible, has recently been exploded by the cytological investigations of Longley and Tourje in America and in practice by several camellia breeders in different parts of the world.

There are records of a nursery firm of Davies having been in business at Wavertree near Liverpool. Gore's *Directory of Liverpool* for the period 1818–29 lists a John Davies, nursery and seedsman of Wavertree. For the years 1832–43 the *Directory* lists a Thomas Davies, nursery and seedsman of Wavertree. From 1845 the *Directory* describes the firm as Thomas Davies & Company, nursery and seedsman, of various addresses in Wavertree Road and Picton Road, Wavertree. The last entry for Thomas Davies and Company is in the *Directory* of 1923, which gives the firm's address as 250, Picton Road, Wavertree.

A correspondent has suggested that the raiser might have been Isaac Davies of Ormskirk, who bred several hybrid shrubs about that time including the well-known *Rhododendron* x 'Praecox', *Azalea x daviesii* and the Davies Hybrid Pernettyas.

I wonder whether any reader can throw any light on this lost camellia. It would appear to have been propagated successfully, not ony by the raiser, but also by the Verschaffelts in their Ghent Camellia nursery. Alexandre Verschaffelt died in April 1850, the year that this particular camellia was described and illustrated in the *Iconographie,* and the family business was carried on by his son Ambroise, who continued publishing regular editions up to 1860. The *Iconographie* was published in monthly fascicles each of four-colour plates with brief descriptions, making forty-eight plates to each annual volume.

The Verschaffelt description of *Camellia* x 'Emperor' published in 1850, is as follows:

'Forte belle irrégularité, à trés grands pétales, serrés, contournés, chiffonnés, diversement groupés, d'un rouge cramoisi foncé, passant presque au blanc vers les bords.

123

Ce Camellia, dans le commerce depuis quelques années déjà, est dû à M. Davies, horticulteur, pres de Liverpool, qui l'a obtenu, nous a t il dit, en fecondant un *C. colulii* par le *reticulata*.

Les individus que nous avon observés chez lui dans le temps avaient deux à trois mètres de hauteur et étaient littéralement couverts de fleurs: sa floraison successive dans nos serres a prouvé que c'est là une variété constante, d'un port superbe et d'une fertilité florale peu ordinaire.'

In recent years several hybrids have been bred in New Zealand by crossing 'Captain Rawes' *reticulata* with *C. saluenensis*. These include:

'Barbara Clark'. A medium large semi-double rose-pink of vigorous and upright growth.

'Bettie Durrant'. Semi-double rose-pink, of erect and compact habit.

'Brian'. Medium large, semi-double, deep pink with silvery cast and compact, erect growth.

'Dr Lesley'. Large semi-double phlox pink with crinkled petals and a lavender cast.

'Fair Lass'. Persian Rose shading to white at centre. Large semi-double.

'Otara Rose'. Very large, semi-double, phlox-pink.

'Phyl Doak'. Bengal Rose, large semi-double flowers. Erect and compact growth.

Camellia x 'Salutation', the forerunner of these hybrids, was destined to become the most controversial camellia in the world, for its parentage was long in dispute. A large pale pink, single to semi-double, with long strap-like petals and of vigorous, open growth, it was bred, along with the famous Williamsii hybrid 'Donation' by Walter Fleming, head gardener to the late Colonel Stephenson R. Clarke, V.M.H. at Borde Hill, near Haywards Heath, Sussex, who claimed that its parentage was *C. saluenensis* x *C. reticulata*. Since Forrest's original introduction of the wild, single form of

C. reticulata did not flower at Caerhays until 1932, the *C. reticulata* named as the male parent could only have been 'Captain Rawes'. Assuming that a seedling takes not less than seven years to flower (unless kept in an artificial environment of high temperatures and prolonged day-length, a process which was not then an established horticultural practice), I calculate the approximate date of the cross to have been prior to 1925. In the *Catalogue of Trees and Shrubs (excluding Rhododendrons) at Borde Hill, Sussex in December 1932,* compiled by Albert Bruce Jackson, A.L.S., one reads on page 50:

'*Camellia speciosa* (Syn. *C. saluenensis*). It is growing on the north side of the Rose Garden wall where it blooms freely and has been hybridised with *C. reticulata. The resulting hybrid bears a double flower of a very pleasing pale pink.*' (Plate 14.)

In spite of Colonel Clarke's insistence on its parentage, many leading authorities discredited his claim because of the highly sterile nature of the pollen of *C. reticulata* 'Captain Rawes', itself somewhat of an enigma.

Although 'Salutation' received an Award of Merit as long ago as 1936 its general release was apparently delayed by the war, so that it received little attention in camellia circles until about 1848. 'Donation' received a similar Award in 1941 but likewise remained relatively unknown until both hybrids were introduced to camellia connoisseurs about the same time. This fact, and their vague similarity, may account for the widely held but erroneous assumption that they must have originated from the same or a similar cross. It should be recalled that the parentage of 'Donation' was recorded as *saluenensis* x *japonica* 'Donckelarii', making it an early member of the 'Williamsii' race of hybrids.

The late C. P. Raffill, then assistant curator at the Royal Botanic Gardens, Kew, wrote to me in 1948 to say that he had been down to Borde Hill with the leading American

125

authority, Dr Harold Hume, to inspect the mother plant of 'Salutation', and that they could find no evidence of *Camellia reticulata* in its foliage or growth habit. In this opinion he was also supported by British camellia expert Robert Sealy. How easy it is to become so convinced of a theory that evidence of a contrary nature is as preaching to the converted. These authorities were so insistent that an error must have occurred in the recording of the cross that eventually even the raiser began to waver under the weight of their evidence.

Because of the very complex processes involved in chromosome counting and the fact that remarkable irregularities occur in the chromosomes of the pollen mother cells of both 'Salutation' and 'Captain Rawes', it is not surprising that early cytological investigations by Dr Janaki Ammal in 1955 and by Mr L. F. La Cour in 1956 were conflicting.

Reporting on their findings in the *Royal Horticultural Society's Rhododendron and Camellia Year Book, 1957,* the late Major George H. Johnstone, V.M.H., of Trewithen, wrote:

'In the light of information which the chromosome count affords we may surely assume with some certainty that the two hybrids 'Donation' and 'Salutation' are sisters of the same breeding, and in support of this assumption we have the opinion of Mr J. R. Sealy, the leading systematic authority on the genus Camellia who, at p. 175 of the Supplement to the R.H.S. Dictionary of Gardening, writes of *C.* 'Salutation' 'thought to be a hybrid of *C. reticulata* x *C. saluenensis* but undoubtedly *C. japonica* x *C. saluenensis,* i.e. *C.* x williamsii'.

In two letters from the late Colonel Stephenson R. Clarke of Borde Hill to the author dated September and October 1948 he refers to a visit to Borde Hill in September of that year by the late Mr C. P. Raffill of Kew and Dr Harold Hume. Both of these had told him that they thought a mistake had been made in attributing 'Salutation' to a cross between *C. saluenensis* and *C. reticulata* and that it should really be attributed to a cross between *C. saluenensis* and *C. japonica* 'Donckelarii' making it a sister seedling to 'Donation'. In the second letter Colonel Stephenson Clarke added 'I must confess they look to me as though they might be such.'

In the pages following Major Johnstone's notes are some contributed on the same topic by the late Mr Francis Hanger, V.M.H., then Curator of the Royal Horticultural Society's Garden at Wisley. He likewise visited Borde Hill to inspect and compare the mother plants of 'Donation' and 'Salutation', accompanied by the Society's senior botanist, Mr N. K. Gould, and came to the conclusion that the former possessed a glossy leaf confirming the parentage of *C. saluenensis* and *C. japonica* 'Donckelarii' and the latter *C.* 'Salutation' possessed a more dull, matt leaf showing distinct resemblance to *reticulata*.

Colonel Stephenson Clarke's version of the parentage of 'Salutation' was stoutly upheld by many other experienced camellia growers. Like most Reticulatas, it is difficult to propagate from cuttings, whereas 'Donation' roots very readily. It has well-spaced, narrow, pointed leathery-textured matt-surfaced leaves with impressed, reticulate venation. Its habit is sparse and erect with the Reticulata tendency to produce only terminal and sub-terminal growth buds. This 'apical dominance' is thought to be due to a large amount of auxins (complex growth-regulating substances) moving down from the apices of the shoots and inhibiting the growth of lateral buds.

The presence of cork warts on or in the leaves seems to indicate that the *saluenensis* parent had some *japonica* blood since these are a character confined to *C. japonica*. They were cited as evidence by the experts who disputed 'Salutation's declared parentage.

127

More recent cytological studies carried out by Longley and Tourje at the instance of the American Camellia Advisory Committee, and reported in the 1960 edition of the *American Camellia Year Book,* leave no doubt that 'Salutation' is indeed a hybrid of *C. saluenensis* x *C. reticulata* 'Captain Rawes'. They found irrefutable proof that 'Salutation' has a chromosome combination identical with that of its putative parent.

The name *C.* x 'Borde Hill Hybrids' has been suggested as a group name for this and any further hybrids of similar parentage. Cornish Camellia breeder Miss Gillian Carlyon has now flowered a hybrid which she bred in 1961 by crossing 'Salutation' with *C. japonica* 'Rosea Simplex', and which she grew in a controlled environment with a twenty-hour daylength for three years. The flowers of this remarkable plant bear a close resemblance to those of *C. reticulata* 'Captain Rawes', thus providing still further proof of the authenticity of 'Salutation's' parentage.

New Zealand Camellia breeder Les Jury has bred 'Grand Jury' from *C. saluenensis* x 'Salutation'. This interesting hybrid resembles an improved 'Salutation' with large semi-double to peony-form flowers, light pink with salmon cast and long elliptical leaves.

'Citation'. This camellia is classed as a 'Williamsii' hybrid by the well-known camellia expert, Mr Charles Puddle, who introduced it from the famous gardens of Lord Aberconway and the National Trust at Bodnant in North Wales. But after very careful scrutiny and consideration I cannot help wondering if it might not be a hybrid of *C. reticulata simplex.*

Firstly, it is remarkably slender and erect in growth with little tendency to produce side branches. This is due to what is termed 'apical dominance', whereby its growth buds are restricted to terminal and sub-terminal leaf axil positions. In 'Citation' this is so pronounced that it contrives to con-

128

ceal its own flower buds, and plants, thought to be budless, suddenly surprise with an unexpected display of large, semi-double, pale pink flowers.

Secondly the leaves of 'Citation' are typical of *C. reticulata*, being narrow, stiff and leathery in texture, with impressed, reticulate venation.

Thirdly there is a pronounced absence of basal leaves on the annual growths, a further factor typical of *C. reticulata* which contributes to the sparse, gaunt appearance of many members of this race.

Fourthly the petals are often bilobed or emarginate at the tips, some having a tendency to form marginal outgrowths and thus becoming irregular in shape. Petaloids tend to appear amongst the stamens and some flowers closely resemble those of the controversial *C.* x 'Salutation'.

Bearing in mind the close similarity between the wild form of *C. saluenensis* and *C. reticulata* which I have referred to elsewhere in these chapters, and the fact that they often grow in close proximity in British gardens, as in the wilds of China, I feel sure that, if the possibility of either of its putative parents having been *C. reticulata simplex* be ruled out, then one of them must have had some unsuspected *reticulata* influence in its make-up.

I hope that this interesting poser will be investigated cytologically in the near future by experts, in the same manner as was the long contested riddle of the parentage of 'Salutation'.

'Barbara Hillier'. This camellia was discovered in the garden of the late Mr J. J. Crosfield at Embley Park near Romsey, Hampshire, by the well-known nurseryman and camellia expert, Mr H. G. Hillier of Winchester, by whom it was purchased and named, and whose firm propagated and distributed it. It bears large, semi-double flowers and was first thought to be a 'Williamsii' hybrid. In his *Revision of the Genus Camellia,* J. Robert Sealy classes 'Barbara Hillier'

129

as a form of *C. heterophylla,* admitting that this has a doubtful right to specific rank since it could well represent a race
of hybrids between *C. reticulata* and *C. japonica.*

THE KUNMING RETICULATAS

The famous plant collector, George Forrest, made several
visits to Yunnan between 1912 and 1930, so it seems strange
that he apparently overlooked the extraordinarily large-
flowered cultivated forms of *C. reticulata* which graced many
of the old temple gardens—or was he professionally preju-
diced to cultivated plants? It seems incredible that he could
have failed to notice that the residents of Kunming had been
selecting and breeding garden forms of *C. reticulata* for
many centuries, during which they had raised variants com-
parable to the cultivars of *C. japonica.* Further introduction
of these into the Western world was delayed until 1948,
when this was achieved first by Dr. W. E. Lammerts of
Descanso Gardens, near Los Angeles, to be followed a year
later by a similar introduction by Mr Ralph Peer, who
probably did more than anyone to popularize camellias
after World War II.

In 1950 some eighteen varieties were described by Dr Yu
at the Royal Horticultural Society's Conference on Camellias and Magnolias. Most of their Chinese names have now
been given English interpretations. All of them are remarkable for the size of their flowers but their growth habit is
inclined to be sparse and slender when grown out of doors,
and they are sensitive to severe cold. They all make excellent
greenhouse plants where height is adequate for their future
development, and then make more robust and bushier
growth, as is demonstrated by the remarkably fine collection
in the Temperate House in the Royal Gardens at Windsor
Great Park. The young foliage of the Kunming Reticulatas
is almost as brilliantly coloured as some forms of *Pieris
formosa.*

Their origin as garden plants dates back over one thousand years, so that they must represent the longest surviving plant cultivars in the world. Because they can only be propagated by grafting they are, in fact, horticultural prolongations of the original plants which first delighted Chinese eyes in the ninth century A.D.

Unfortunately considerable confusion arose either in the course of their importation or during subsequent relabelling, propagation and distribution in America. These mistakes in identification now appear to have been largely sorted out by camellia expert Colonel T. Durrant in New Zealand, whose findings are published in the 1968 *Rhododendron and Camellia Year Book* of the Royal Horticultural Society. He reported that although some twenty named varieties were supposed to have been imported into America in 1948, it has now been shown that many of these are identical, so that the number of different cultivars was in fact considerably fewer. Plate 5 shows a typical bloom.

The following are some of the best varieties of the Kunming Reticulatas:

'Crimson Robe'. A very large semi-double with crinkled, creped, waxy petals. Growth is vigorous and spreading.

'Cornelian'. Bears large, irregular, peony-form flowers with thick, crinkled, turkey-red petals, striped and blotched white. A vigorous and compact grower, mid-season.

'Pagoda'. Has turned out to be the same form as was introduced by Robert Fortune a century earlier, when it was named 'Flore Pleno'. It is now usually known in British gardens and nurseries as 'Robert Fortune'. (Plate 4.)

'Professor Tsai'. Semi-double rose-pink with undulated petals.

'Purple Gown'. Very large double, imbricated to incomplete double.

'Shot Silk'. Bears large, loose, semi-double flowers with bright pink waxy petals.

Most of these cultivars are now on trial in English gardens,

131

but it is too soon to forecast which will rank as good garden plants, though all are doubtless excellent under glass. It will be interesting to see whether any of them proves as rugged or long-lived as either of the introductions of over a century ago. They seem to prefer maximum exposure to sunlight.

Many seedlings of the Kunming Reticulata have been recorded recently in California resulting from self-pollinations (e.g. 'Lila Naff' from 'Butterfly Wings', 'Mandalay Queen' from 'Tali Queen', 'Rhonda Kerr', 'Janet' and 'Imperial Chang' from 'Cornelian' ('Chang's Temple'). Among those raised from controlled crossings is Howard Asper's 'Mouchang' ('Cornelian' x 'Moutancha').

Already American camellia breeders have raised several new hybrids from the Kunming Reticulatas among which are:

'Buddha'. Perhaps the finest of all, a slender, erect grower producing immense, semi-double blossoms composed of a swirling mass of waxy rose-pink petals, raised by crossing *C. reticulata* 'Early Peach Blossom' with *C. pitardii* var. *yunnanica.*

'Carl Tourje'. A hybrid between the latter species and 'Cornelian'. It is a large semi-double, soft pink, its wavy petals having deeper pink undertones. Its growth is reported to be vigorous and erect.

CAMELLIA JAPONICA x C. RETICULATA

Three putative hybrids between *C. japonica* and *C. reticulata* have been raised by David L. Feathers in California using *C. reticulata* 'Crimson Robe' as the pollen parent. They have been named 'Fairy Wings' (semi-double white with undulating petals and stamens).

'Fluted Orchid'. Of similar parentage and flower form but pale orchid pink in colour.

'White Orchid'. Has long twisted strap-like petals with a

tinge of pink, having the same parentage as above.

In April 1968 Mr Frank Maitland of Sylmar, California, registered two putative hybrids of this parentage: 'John Taylor' (Reg. No. 1013) with very large dark red flowers 6-6½ inches in diameter and of considerable depth, and 'Pink Sparkle' (Reg. No. 1030), a very large sparkling pink with yellow anthers. He is reported to have named other putative hybrids of this parentage 'Bernadette Karsten', 'Silver Mist', 'Temple Mist' and 'Descanso Mist'. The flowers of some of these are said to 'exude fluorescence' like the effect of an over-spray. From the stable of Howard Asper at Escondido, California, comes 'Valentine's Day' (*C. reticulata* 'Crimson Robe' x *C. japonica* 'Tiffany', following the fine hybrid bearing his name which resulted from *C. reticulata* 'Lionhead' x *C. japonica* 'Coronation'. Frank Pursel of Oakland, California, is reported to have crossed *C. reticulata* 'Cornelian' with *C. japonica* 'Mrs D. W. Davis'.

I have not yet set eyes on any of these putative hybrids but I suggest that it is only right that they be treated with the same scepticism as that which haunted 'Salutation' for so many years, until their chromosome count has been checked. However careful a breeder may be to control and record his hand-pollinations and protect the treated flowers from contamination, the chance of some seed production occurring through apomixis should be anticipated, especially where the pollen of the male parent is known to be highly sterile.

Camellia cytologists believe that some putative hybrids are, in fact, apomicts. Through the physiological process known as *apomixis*, plant cells are stimulated to develop embryos, not through physical contact with pollen nuclei, but merely by reason of proximity of pollen nuclei. Therefore a seedling resulting from apogamy inherits only the characters of the seed parent.

Other recent hybrids of *Camellia reticulata* include 'China Lady' (*C. reticulata* 'Buddha' x *C. granthaniana*), a very

133

large semi-double orchid-pink, mid-season, bred by Nuccio's Nursery of Altadena, California. Hybrids between *C. sasanqua* 'Narumigata' and *C. reticulata* have been bred by Howard Asper of Escondido, California, and these first flowered in 1960. Popularly referred to as 'the three girls', they comprise 'Dream Girl' (*C. reticulata* 'Buddha' x *C. sasanqua* 'Narumigata'), large geranium lake, cup-shaped with high centre, 'Flower Girl' (*C. sasanqua* 'Narumigata' x *C. reticulata* 'Lionhead'), bearing 5½-inch diameter flowers coloured spinel-pink. 'Show Girl', of the same parentage as 'Flower Girl', has flatter scarlet flowers with petals of satiny appearance. The flowers of all three are reported to be borne singly along the branches in long succession from early autumn through early winter. They certainly sound most attractive additions to the camellia repertoire.

The double Reticulatas make excellent wall plants, growing most luxuriantly when facing north or west. On southerly aspects they may flower more freely but their growth tends to be much slower because of the hotter and therefore drier conditions. East-facing walls are suitable in districts above normal spring ground-frost levels or where flowers are effectively screened from early sun by hillsides, trees or adjacent buildings.

Unlike other camellias they show little tendency to produce a second growth flush in July so that their rate of development is consequently much slower. The bases of their annual growths are leafless and they tend to shed foliage from their older branches. These factors contribute to their relative sparseness of growth. They tend also to produce relatively few side shoots because their growth buds are nearly all terminal and sub-terminal. This characteristic is termed 'apical dominance'.

A word here about grafting. It is remarkable how some garden owners boast that they would not have a grafted plant on their premises, often where fruit trees and roses have been grown for generations on various understocks. Clearly the Double Reticulatas are not for them, since they are only likely to be available as grafted plants. Modern propagation techniques make it possible to graft Double Reticulatas directly onto pot-established understocks of *C. japonica* or *C. x williamsii*. Unfortunately the closely related *C. saluenensis* and *C. reticulata simplex* which seed so freely and could be readily mass-produced, have, in my experience, proved unsatisfactory as understocks, but in New Zealand Colonel Durrant has found them superior to *C. japonica*. Seasonal observations of their meristem activity, now being carried out for me at Exeter University, may throw some light on this problem.

Previously it was found necessary to graft them by the approach method, also known as inarching. This consists of side-grafting suitably placed shoots onto pot-established understocks without severing them from the parent plant until an adequate union has developed. It entails very careful attention to watering, since the stocks are frequently positioned on staging or other supports in order to make best use of suitable growths as scions, the basal growths usually being insufficient in number from a nurseryman's point of view. There is also considerable skill necessary to wean the grafted plants after severance from the parent.

Continental nurserymen appear to favour saddle grafting, whereby the understocks are cut back to within 2 inches of the roots, the remainder of the shoot being cut to a wedge-shaped point over which the scion is fitted, after making an upward cut of equivalent length through its base. The reverse of this procedure, whereby the scion is cut to form a wedge-shaped point, which is fitted into a downward cut into the centre of the short remaining portion of the under-stock, is less popular because water is liable to trickle into the union of stock and scion, whilst it is encouraged to drain away with the former type.

135

British propagators favour side or cleft grafting, a method which does not entail the virtual destruction of the under-stock. Details of these methods of grafting are described in detail in the chapter on propagation.

With Reticulatas the two-year wood is preferred to scions of the previous year's growth, as is customary with other camellias. The Kunming Reticulatas may also be tip-grafted in August using half-ripe shoot tips as scions and cleft grafting them onto the tops of pot-established rooted cuttings. The newly grafted plants may be completely enclosed in polythene bags where no propagating frame is available.

CAMELLIA x 'EMPEROR'

My quest for this Camellia came to an unexpected conclusion when, shortly after the text of this chapter had gone to the publishers, I received a letter from Mr George E. Newton, camellia-fancier, hybridist and propagator, of Fayetteville, North Carolina, U.S.A., who is also a collector of camellia literature. Mr Newton had suddenly come across my notes on *Camellia* x 'Emperor' which were published in the 1968 edition of the Royal Horticultural Society's *Rhododendron and Camellia Year Book*.

He enclosed an illustrated leaflet which had been printed and circulated by the late Robert O. Rubel, Jr. of the 'Long-view' Camellia Nursery, Crichton Station, Alabama, U.S.A., probably in 1947, for the sole purpose of re-introducing this camellia to his American clientele. The front page depicts a monochrome of Verschaffelt's plate 11 against the background of an oriental court on which costumed dignitaries and courtiers are regarding the bloom with respect and awe. On the inside page is a reproduction of Verschaffelt's original text with an English translation. On the opposite page is a photograph of a flower of 'Emperor' which Rubel took at "Longview", 'on February 6, 1942, thirty days after the parent plant, growing outdoors without protection, had been subjected to 18°F, temperature, or 14 degrees below freezing'. He reported that plants grown outdoors in 5-gallon cans started to bloom on 21 November in 1945 and on 17 November in 1946, and that they continued to flower until warm weather in March. He said that the flowers were 4½-5½ inches across and that the earlier ones, on plants growing in shade, were light rose pink with variable white markings. Plants exposed to lower temperatures and full winter sunshine produced darker red, distinctly veined flowers with white markings.

On the back of the leaflet Rubel printed several testimonials from his clients concerning *Camellia* x 'Emperor', and it is of interest that their dates varied from March 1939 to January 1946. He claimed that he located this camellia on 13 March 1931 in a garden near Mobile and propagated from it under his Lot No. 109 in the summer of 1932. It would appear that he resold the very bushy 5-foot specimen camellia to a South Carolina customer for $250 and a photograph of this plant is shown on the leaflet with the above information as a caption, adding: 'In the maze of conflicting Camellia names, documentary proof, verified by rights of priority, as evidence supplied from Verschaffelt's monograph, proves the accuracy in identification as the true *Camellia* "Emperor".'

THE GILLIAN CARLYON CAMELLIA HYBRIDS

During the past decade there has been a veritable explosion of new camellia varieties raised in the United States and recorded by the American Camellia Society. The reason for this is largely climatic but partly know-how.

Climatically most of the camellia-growing areas in America have a higher average temperature at blossom time than is experienced in the British Isles, which take longer to

137

warm up in the spring because of cooling winds and high humidity derived from the surrounding seas. Camellia pollen does not usually germinate in temperatures below 60°F and resulting failures in hand pollinations must have deterred many would-be amateur hybridists. Know-how is readily available to American camellia enthusiasts, not only through their camellia clubs and societies but also through the horticultural faculties at several of their universities.

Miss Gillian Carlyon started a small camellia nursery in the walled garden of her Cornish family estate at Tregrehan near St Austell in 1950, at first propagating from camellias which had flourished there for over a century, many of which had attained tree-like dimensions.

Apart from acquiring the best of the British-raised hybrids, she also imported from the United States new varieties which had won the highest awards in American camellia competitions and decided to experiment with camellia breeding herself. She started by inscribing the known chromosome counts, of the species which she grew, on the wall of her camellia house but later decided to disregard the barriers suggested by such knowledge and use her own intuition as a guide.

She commenced her pollinations early in 1960, at first using a pot-established specimen of *C. saluenensis* as the female parent, and met with immediate failure due to the low atmospheric temperature which prevailed in her unheated greenhouse.

Know-how was acquired by diligent reading of camellia publications and a flair for improvisation. Having discovered the cause of her failure she proceeded to enclose each pollinated flower in a large polythene bag into the neck of which she tied an electric lamp socket housing a 60-watt bulb. The heat output from the lamp raised the temperature sufficiently to germinate the pollen grains, which she had introduced onto the styles from the flower of a selected parent, and, although some leaf scorch resulted, the desired effect was achieved after continuing this treatment for two or three days. Then she repeated the process on further flowers and also began using other plants as female parents, always carefully emasculating their flowers to avoid contamination with their own pollen.

The original metal tags on which she had recorded the crosses were carefully segregated with the resulting camellia apples as soon as these were ripe enough to harvest. The seeds which each contained, varying from one to eight in number, were sown, as soon as ripe, in small pots marked with their original labels. The pots were then plunged in a mixture of peat and sand in a propagating case with gentle bottom heat and then followed an anxious wait for germination.

As soon as the seedlings were large enough to handle she followed the latest procedure by removing them from their pots and severing the lower half of their tap roots prior to re-potting them and returning them to their heated plunge beds.

She then rigged a row of 250-watt billiard room lamps and suspended them about a foot above the seedlings. These lights were controlled by a time-switch to provide extended day-length from sunset to within four hours of daybreak, and maintained a high temperature additional to the thermostatically controlled bottom heat of the frame. The whole set-up was draped with clear polythene curtains to maintain maximum heat and humidity.

She fed the seedlings from the outset with a very weak solution combining 'Wellgrow' and urea, applied in small doses as frequently as two or three times a week. Soon they began to grow rapidly in their carefully controlled environment and she had to raise the high-powered lamps to avoid scorching their shoots. As often as their roots began to emerge through the drainage holes in the pots they were transferred to larger sizes until, at the end of three years, they had reached the limits of their environment, the taller growers having been topped to avoid scorching their leaves through contact with the lamps.

She then decided to plant them out in the floor of the adjacent greenhouse where a crop of tomatoes had just been cleared. As yet there was no sign of the long-awaited flower buds. Some plants which she ring-barked at the base with a sharp knife were apparently unaffected by such treatment. She had trebled their initial rate of growth but it remained to be seen what effect this would have on their flowering age, which is normally eight to fifteen years.

The following spring her first seedling flowered when four years old. It was a cross between two Japonica cultivars, the fine single red 'Juno' crossed with double bicolour 'The Mikado', which Miss Carlyon had selected as a male parent because of its freedom of flowering as a young plant. The resulting bloom was sensational and quite unlike either parent, being a large, double anemone- to peony-form with rosy red petals. A second seedling of this cross commenced to flower a year or so later as a large semi-double crimson with bold, twisted petals and flared yellow stamens intermingled with petaloids. These two seedlings alone would have been rich reward for any camellia breeder but even more surprises were in store for her. The following year several other seedlings began to flower; C. japonica 'Juno' x C. williamsii 'Donation' produced a plant with extra bold foliage and large single pink flowers freely produced named 'William Carlyon'.

Two almost identical seedlings resulted from a cross between C. saluenensis and C. japonica 'Adolphe Audusson', both bearing a remarkable likeness to 'Donation'. One of these has now been named 'Edward Carlyon' after her great-great-grandfather.

Other seedlings of the same cross have flowered quite differently, one being an extraordinarily large salmon-pink, semi-double shaped like its well-known male parent. Yet another from the same cross is a fully double silvery pink, whilst 'Pamela McLean' is a handsome semi-double of a pale shade of dog-rose pink.

Launching out into the sphere of the unpredictable she succeeded in crossing C. *japonica* 'Juno' with C. *heterophylla* 'Barbara Hillier' to give 'Belinda Carlyon', a hybrid with large single rosy-red flowers with darker veins and pink stamen filaments. A second seedling has produced larger flowers with fewer petals.

Gillian Carlyon was not numbered amongst those who doubted the declared parentage of C. x 'Salutation', and her *pièce de resistance* is undoubtedly her hybrid of 'Salutation' x *japonica* 'Rosea Simplex', which, as stated in an earlier chapter, has the same colour and fluted petal formation as C. *reticulata* 'Captain Rawes', thus adding one more link to the chain of evidence proving 'Salutation's long-disputed parentage. This is named 'Tristam Carlyon' after her brother. She now awaits the flowering of a number of 'Salutation' seedlings which she has raised from natural pollinations under glass.

C. *saluenensis* x C. *japonica* 'C. M. Wilson' has produced a hybrid with large, semi-double, cup-shaped, pink flowers and remarkable, shiny, reticulated leaves, quite unlike those of either parent. This hybrid she has named 'Jenefer Carlyon'.

A hybrid between C. *reticulata simplex* and C. *japonica* 'Juno' produced a plant with most unusual stamenless flowers of a deep pink shade. This she has named 'A. L. Rowse'.

The last of her seedlings to start flowering, then photographed by the author in March 1967, is 'Rupert Carlyon', a remarkable hybrid between C. *williamsii* 'J. C. Williams' and C. *japonica* 'Adolphe Audusson', with flowers most aptly described as resembling large, double white begonias. I have earlier referred to some camellias having flowers with in-

141

curved petals as being 'ranunculus form' but the flowers of this hybrid can best be described as 'begonia form'. The plant has an open, spreading habit with attractively bullated foliage. All other seedlings of this cross have produced white flowers likewise, being mostly single and apparently deriving their colour from the Japonica parent 'J. C. Williams'.

Gillian Carlyon is extremely modest over her achievements. No doubt much of her original excitement has gradually waned with the inevitable lapse of time though made much shorter by the methods which she adopted. It is remarkable that, so far, four out of five of her seedlings are worthy of retention, a much higher proportion than one might have anticipated. She still awaits the flowering of about a hundred and fifty crosses which she has been growing without artificial aids, having selected only seedlings of distinctive appearance for the controlled environment treatment.

It might be well to mention here that seedlings raised by fertilizing flowers of one variety of, say, *C. japonica* with pollen from another of the same species are termed 'crosses', whilst true hybrids are the result of fertilization of one species or hybrid with pollen from a different one.

So far Miss Carlyon has only flowered her new hybrids and crosses under glass but she now proposes to test their qualities as garden plants, and we await the result of these trials with considerable interest.

Cornwall has long been famous for its camellias. Gillian Carlyon has created magnificent new ones which will certainly do much to maintain the future camellia prestige of this delectable duchy.

XI

Diseases, Pests and Maladies

Camellias are usually remarkably robust and healthy plants, but the few troubles which affect them are briefly described and remedies suggested here.

DISEASES

FLOWER BLIGHT (*Sclerotinia camelliae*). As far as is known, this disease has not established itself in British gardens but it is reported to be very damaging in parts of America, and care should be taken so that any original outbreak can be promptly dealt with. It was first introduced into California from Japan about 1938 and has since spread over a wide area. It is recognizable from the appearance of small, irregular, brownish specks on the petals of opening flowers. In warm, humid weather these specks rapidly enlarge and unite to form large brown blotches involving whole petals and eventually whole flowers. It does not affect the bush in any other way. The disease is transferred to the soil on fallen blossoms whence fresh spores appear each spring and are carried onto the opening flowers by air currents. There appears to be no secondary spread from flower to flower. Nurseries in affected areas are advised not to allow any of their plants to blossom. In America the transfer of plants from state to state is now forbidden unless all soil is washed from their roots. The disease is not carried on scions or cuttings unless these have open flowers on them. Control

143

measures include the regular burning or deep burial of all fallen flowers and the application of a proved fungicidal chemical to the soil beneath all camellia bushes. Efforts are being made to perfect a systematic fungicide that could be absorbed by plants to provide immunity over the critical period for infection.

CAMELLIA FLOWER GALL (*Exobasidium nudum* Shirai) (syn. *Exobasidium camelliae* Shirai). At the beginning of July 1967 my son Andrew discovered several remarkably grotesque white fungal growths on the tips of four shoots on a plant of *C. japonica* 'Adolphe Audusson' some ten miles from our Truro nurseries. These resembled white puff-balls but varied considerably in shape and size and, upon closer examination, it became evident that the fungus had developed on flower buds and flowers, one of which had reached a mature condition before becoming engulfed. They had remained on the plant at least two months beyond the normal blossom shedding period.

The affected shoots were carefully removed and photographed before being placed separately in polythene bags and forwarded to the area plant pathological laboratory for examination, where the cause was identified as *Exobasidium camelliae*.

This grotesque disease is fortunately very rare in Western countries though not uncommon in Japan, where it is known as 'Moti-byo', or Leaf and Stem Gall. Since the fungus produces such revolting growths, which completely enshroud the flowers and flower buds with white puff-ball-like coatings, I think it more appropriate to refer to it here as Camellia Flower Gall. The only previous record of this disease in England was in June 1944, when an abnormal, diseased flower was sent to Kew from a garden at Handcross in Sussex.

The responsible fungus is described under *Exobasidium camelliae* in the *Transactions of the British Mycological*

144

Society, Vol. 29, 1946. This name was corrected to *Exobasidium nudum* (Shirai) S. Ito by Dr Kenichi Shirahama, Specialist of Plant Diseases of the Economic Affairs Bureau of the Tokyo Metropolitan Government, to whom I wrote for further information. He said that 'Moti-byo' of Camellias makes gall on leaves, stems and flower buds. The damage which we observed was confined to the flowers in various stages of their development. In 1962 the disease was reported in New Zealand (*Trans. Roy. Soc. N.Z.,* Bot. 1, N.S. 261–2).

The cause of such isolated infections is difficult to understand until one realizes that fungal spores are known to travel thousands of miles in the upper atmosphere. The spores of this fungus are probably only active at blossom time, when several successive sprayings with Zineb plus a suitable wetter are recommended. The related disease on rhododendrons and evergreen azaleas can be controlled by spraying at weekly intervals with five grams of Captan per litre of water commencing as soon as growth appears in the spring.

HONEY OR BOOTLACE FUNGUS (*Armillaria mellia*). This scourge operates underground, at first living on the decomposing roots of dead and felled trees and shrubs. It is therefore most likely to be present in woodland gardens or on sites recently cleared of timber. This fungus sends up toadstools with honey-coloured cups and brown scales, on long yellow stalks in late summer.

Attacked plants suddenly collapse and die for no apparent reason until a close examination of their roots reveals the tell-tale, black, bootlace-like rhizomorphs of the fungus. It can be also diagnosed by lifting off a portion of bark from the collar of the plant, just below ground level, where it usually reveals itself as thin, white, fan-like sheets of mycelium. Camellias seem to be less susceptible to attack than rhododendrons.

The recommended cure is some form of volatile liquid soil fumigation with a proven chemical such as formaldehyde, or perhaps the new German WN12 when it becomes more readily available, but site preparation and application must be thorough and in accordance with the manufacturer's instructions. Unfortunately the fumes might prove fatal to adjacent plants whose roots are within the treated area.

Successful control of *Armillaria* by drenching the roots of a number of different species of woody plants with a creosote (of unrecorded British Standard Specification), also with creosote BSS 3051 (1958), was reported by Victoria Bray of Tillingbourne Cottage, Shene, Nr Guildford, Surrey, England, in *Journal of the Royal Horticultural Society* (Jan. 1970), pp. 27, 95. More recently a proprietory liquid has been put on the market under the registered trade name *Armillatox.*

Armillatox is a phenolic emulsion for dilution at the rate of twelve times its volume of water. The solution should be applied to thoroughly drench the roots. The manufacturers, recommend that, when dealing with infected trees and large shrubs, a series of holes be made in a staggered pattern around the collar area so that the solution comes into direct contact with the mycelium of the attacking fungus. It would appear to be toxic to non-woody plants (i.e. bulbs and herbaceous plants). The manufacturers are Armillatox Ltd, Henley, Fernhurst, Nr Haslemere, Surrey, England.

LEAF SPOT (*Pestalozzia guepini* and *Phyllosticta camelliae*). Some authorities consider that both these organisms are, in fact, weak parasites which do not attack the leaves until these have been superficially damaged by sunburn, chemicals, polluted drip from overhanging trees or by minor mechanical injury. Faulty glass will sometimes produce lens-like concentrations of sunlight which gives rise to these symptoms appearing on plants in the same position in a greenhouse each summer. The responsible fungus causes

146

the appearance of brown spots which resemble scorch marks. These later become greyish with tiny, black, dot-like fruits sprinkled over their surfaces. The picking and burning of affected leaves is usually an adequate method of control.

SOOTY MOULD (*Capriodium* and *Meliola spp*). This is caused by a fungus which forms a black, soot-like film on leaves which have been fouled by the 'honeydew' excreted by insect pests. The effect is only superficial but it is most unsightly, and interferes with light penetration and photosynthesis. Both surfaces of the leaves should be sponged off with a soapy mixture to which a suitable insecticide such as Malathion has been added, taking the precautions recommended by the manufacturers. At the same time remove all weak, overcrowded shoots and dead wood which make eradication of the responsible pest difficult and may give rise to re-infestation. (See also under PESTS.)

VIRUS DISEASES. These may be responsible for the yellow leaf-mottling of some camellias and also petal variegation whereby some coloured varieties produce flowers with white flecks. Although virus infection is transmitted from stock to scion and vice versa on grafted plants it does not appear to be spread by normal handling or by insects. Excessively variegated foliage is often weak and inclined to scorch badly in hot sunlight but it can look very attractive when suitably blended into floral arrangements. Some forms of leaf-mottling are thought to be due to somatic mutations which the plant has inherited. Well-known camellias inclined to leaf-mottling include the Japonica varieties 'Elegans', 'Imbricata Rubra' and 'Preston Rose', and *C. vernalis* 'Dawn'.

PESTS OF CAMELLIAS

Insect pests are usually more troublesome under glass. Plants grown in the open in British gardens are seldom attacked with sufficient severity to warrant attention, although instances of attack by scale insects and mealy bugs with subsequent sooty mould have been noted by us on outdoor plants in some of the milder counties.

APHIDES. These are only likely to prove troublesome under glass and confine their attentions almost entirely to the young shoots, where they are readily seen feeding in large colonies. They can be controlled by spraying with almost any good insecticide. There is usually only one main infestation during the period of active growth.

ANTS. These often swarm over plants infested with aphides and mealy bugs because they are fond of the honeydew excreted by them. They are known to transport these pests from one plant to another. Their presence on camellias should therefore be viewed with suspicion.

BIRDS. It may appear strange to include our feathered friends in such a list but they are often very destructive to camellia blossoms, especially the earlier forms of *C. saluenensis* and single-flowered cultivars of *C. x williamsii*. A number of different birds are blamed for the damage which is usually restricted to the uppermost petals of the horizontally opposed flower buds just before they are due to open. It would appear that the birds are after the nectar within the stamen cylinder, as they do not seem to eat any of the floral parts. Some blame tits, others sparrows, whilst bullfinches may not be blameless and are more difficult to detect with their insidious manner of feeding. The damage reminds one of that inflicted on the flowers of broad beans by bumblebees. Bird-repellents appear to have a very fleeting effect and leave whitish stains on the foliage. Tufts of bright blue cloth or paper strung close to or across the top of the bush usually act as an effective scare but are unsightly.

148

CAPSID BUG (*Lygus pabulinus*). The common green capsid can cause considerable disfigurement to camellias by puncturing the terminal growth buds in early summer, the damage becoming more apparent as the leaves expand. Attacks appear to be sudden and sporadic. Timely dusting with D.D.T. is recommended.

GLASSHOUSE RED SPIDER (*Tetranychus telarius*). Though usually associated with dry atmospheric conditions under glass there is no doubt that some strains of this microscopic pest can tolerate extremes of humidity. The adults are virtually invisible to the naked eye, but their presence can be confirmed on the undersides of the leaves with the aid of a lens. They vary in redness according to age, and protect their feeding grounds with fine web-like coverings which makes effective spraying difficult. The damage manifests itself through a rusty discoloration of the leaves.

Since control measures only affect the live insects it is essential to repeat them two or three times at intervals of seven to ten days in order to dispose of fresh generations which hatch out from eggs immune to treatment.

Derris sprays and Azobenzene smokes are most effective. The latter are available as squib-like generators or combustible tablets, according to the size of the greenhouse.

MEALY BUGS (*Pseudococcus spp*). These are sometimes a nuisance under glass and have also been reported on plants in mild localities out of doors, especially against walls. The symptoms usually include the development of sooty mould on the leaves, and, upon closer inspection, clusters of pink, mealy-covered bugs can be observed beneath the leaves and clustered at the leaf axils and stem junctions. This pest is more difficult to eradicate than scale insects since remnants may have to be brushed out of branch crevices after the leaves have been cleaned by sponging and spraying with

149

Malathion, paying particular attention to their undersurfaces. Malathion should not be applied to very young foliage as it tends to burn.

MICE, MOLES AND SQUIRRELS. These sometimes cause damage to young plants. Mice and squirrels may ring-bark camellias whilst moles, and sometimes ants, can cause losses through loosening the soil beneath and around roots during periods of prolonged drought.

NEMATODES (*Eelworms*). A number of different species of these minute organisms are known to attack the roots of camellias. It is sound policy to buy camellias from a nursery which grows them in sterilized composts to avoid possible contamination.

SCALE INSECTS (*Coccus hesperidium* and *Pulvinaria floccifera*). The former, soft scale, may attack plants growing in protected parts of the garden, especially against walls, and usually when in unthrifty conditions due to lack of summer soil moisture or the alkaline effects of adjacent masonry.

The latter is cushion scale, which also occasionally attacks camellias. Attacks by scale insects are commoner under glass where they are usually followed by the appearance of sooty mould on the upper surfaces of the leaves fouled by excreted fluids. Examination of the undersurfaces of infected leaves reveals flat, elongated disc-like insects adhering limpet fashion. They are only slightly mobile and therefore relatively easy to control by the same method as described for mealy bugs.

WEEVILS (Vine Weevil (*Otiorrhynchus sulcatus*) and Clay-coloured Weevil (*Otiorrhynchus simularis*)). Damage caused by these pests is two-fold and can be fatal especially among container-grown plants under glass. Their white maggots feed on the roots and usually kill camellias by eating away the collars of the plants immediately below soil level.

Whenever a camellia dies suddenly for no obvious reason it is wise to examine the roots and surrounding soil carefully for signs of fat, white grubs about half an inch in length. Also examine the collar between roots and main stem for bark injury.

The second type of damage is caused by nocturnal feeding of the imago beetles, which eat away the edges of young leaves, thus causing disfigurement which remains apparent for the three-year duration normal to camellia foliage.

Apart from strict greenhouse hygiene these pests can be controlled by watering with mercuric perchloride, or by dusting with Aldrin or D.D.T. powder and watering it in. Small traces of D.D.T. or Aldrin should be added to the potting compost at the rate of 2 ounces per bushel. Strains of weevil have developed which have become immune to some of these materials, so it pays to ring the changes and not rely consistently on any one of them. In the open, damage is more likely to occur in old gardens where there is ample cover for pests. Established plants should be dusted with D.D.T. powder as soon as the first sign of leaf damage appears. The beetles can be trapped in the same way as earwigs, by placing wads of hessian or paper or corrugated cardboard for them to hide in. These should be examined each morning and the sheltering weevils destroyed.

MALADIES OF CAMELLIAS

There are several minor ailments which are purely physiological being due to neither pests nor diseases.

BUD DROP. This phenomenon is usually associated with wide fluctuations in soil moisture or temperature. It is most likely to occur on plants grown in containers or against walls, especially those facing away from rain-bearing winds. Close proximity to trees, especially in low-rainfall areas, may also cause this trouble. A few varieties appear prone to this defect when grown out of doors in some areas but they will flower normally when grown under glass.

In some seasons, very late blooming varieties may start into growth just as their flower buds are about to open and these are shed in consequence.

Plants grown in containers may suffer from root dryness in spite of regular watering. This happens when the whole of the root and soil mass shrinks away from the sides of the container so that water simply pours down the cavity without penetrating the root-ball.

Artificial rain-type irrigation is often rather deceptive. It is usually advisable to leave such irrigators in one position for several hours to secure adequate penetration. Where the soil has become very dry it is better to leave a hose slowly trickling on to the roots of such plants for a considerable period, say once every seven to ten days to ensure deep moisture penetration.

CHLOROSIS. This term implies a yellowing or blanching of the leaves of a plant and is usually an indication of a trace-element deficiency. It is often difficult to correct and it may be necessary to persist with several different applications of the same or different chemicals before the plant shows much sign of improvement. It is usually best to transfer the plant to a fresh site since soils vary considerably within a short distance and simply a change of aspect may prove beneficial. Even large camellias will transplant safely when quite dormant, but it is a good idea first to remove completely all weak and overcrowded branches since, by so doing, the reduced amount of foliage will transpire less moisture and safe re-establishment is more certain. Although it is unwise to attempt to bare-root the plant, at least part of the rootball will fall away and more may be carefully teased out so that immediate contact with fresh soil can be made with the feeding roots. Be extra-careful to avoid planting too deeply. The new site should first be liberally dressed with old manure supplemented with several handfuls of balanced fertilizer. Bonemeal is not ideal since it contains calcium and lacks potash. Applications of weathered soot have been proved a reliable tonic for sickly camellias whilst 'Epsom Salts will correct chlorosis induced by magnesium deficiency if sprayed or watered on the foliage in weak solution. Iron chelates, of the kind recommended for treating alkaline soils, may also prove effective if used according to the manufacturers' instructions. A healthy camellia retains its leaves for three years, so it may take that time for a plant to lose all signs of chlorosis.

CORKY EXCRESCENSES AND LEAF SCURF. The leaves of some camellias develop small, dark-brown, corky scabs, usually crescent-shaped on the upper surfaces of the leaves. This occurs most often on 'Adolphe Audusson', which has very heavily textured, dark, glossy foliage. Similar outgrowths, known as camellia leaf scurf, are sometimes formed on the undersurfaces of leaves, especially on Reticulatas.

The cause of both conditions is generally considered to be a temporary imbalance between photosynthesis and assimilation within the affected leaves, causing isolated leaf cells to swell and burst and then turn brown and lignify. Apart from the minor disfigurement, these corky scabs do not appear to be in any way detrimental to the plants affected.

LEAF SCORCH. This involves the formation of brown patches of dead tissue and is usually caused by sun damage through

153

water droplets and is most likely to occur on plants in a dessicated condition. Moral: always water the roots copiously before spraying the foliage.

MARGINAL NECROSIS. Burning or browning of the leaf margins is usually a sign of root injury through over-deep cultivations close to the plants or an application of fertilizer in too great a concentration or when surrounding soil lacks moisture to help to dilute it. The wisest treatment is to leave a hose trickling into the rootball of the plant for several hours in order to wash away the concentration of mineral salts which have caused the trouble. Over-deep cultivations can be averted by winter applications of a mulch or top dressing of bulky organic material which should extend outwards as much as the spread of the branches and be added to annually but never dug in. Alternatively the bushes may be underplanted with suitable ground-cover plants, a selection of which is discussed in the following chapter.

XII

Plant Associates for Camellias and Their Landscape Usage

In nature, one rarely finds a tree or shrub which has no lesser plant or plants growing at its foot and within the spread of its roots. It is therefore natural for plants of low, spreading habit to live in company, and usually in harmony, with those of taller stature.

Quite apart from the fact that bare earth is an eyesore which good gardeners seek to clothe as quickly as possible, most ground-cover plants effectively shade the roots of their taller neighbours and help to prevent the germination of seedling weeds, the eradication of which usually entails a loosening of the surface of the soil with the attendant risk of damage to the feeding roots through dessication or mechanical injury.

Ideal ground-cover plantings should have a recessive nature, never becoming sufficiently dominant to deprive the master plants of adequate light, air and moisture for normal healthy growth. (I am using the term 'master plant' rather than 'host plant' since the latter adjective is already widely used in horticulture to denote plants which harbour and support insects, fungi or parasitic plants.)

It is also desirable that the ground-cover plantings should contribute to the main display of the master plants by providing blendings or harmonious contrasts of colour in flowers, fruit or foliage, or a combination of two or even three of these characters. In this connection do not be misled by

155

the oft-expressed fallacy that flower colours never clash because some of them positively shriek at one another.

Alternatively, ground-covering plants can provide colour and interest before or after the main display of the master plants. This is most desirable in a small garden whilst the former criterion is best sought after in larger plantings, or where colour is required only for one part of the year, as in the garden of a seasonal residence.

Since camellias are the master plants which we are considering here, it is important to have some idea of their future shape, which may not be obvious whilst they are very young. Obviously the most effective under-plantings are those which remain very low and prostrate around tall, erect camellias. Fortunately there are many camellias with this habit of growth, some of which have been fully described in the earlier chapters. Where camellias of a more spreading, bushy habit are to be under-planted, the associate plantings should be truly recessive so that they become swamped and die off as soon as they are overgrown by the master plants.

First let us consider ground-cover plants suitable for associating with camellias to augment their flower display. These will have to flower or bear contrasting foliage in the late winter and early spring whilst the master plants are flowering. A plant which immediately comes to mind is the variegated Yellow Archangel (*Lamium galeobdolon* 'Variegatum'), a vigorous ground-creeper with aluminium markings 'painted' on the upper surfaces of its bright green leaves. Coinciding with the peak of the camellia season, it produces attractive spikes of golden nettle flowers on short, erect stems just long enough to pick and use in a spring flower arrangement. It spreads well, usually rooting as it grows yet not difficult to eradicate if need be.

Another plant of similar habit is the Lesser Periwinkle (*Vinca minor*), which is available in a variety of forms, all of them of neat appearance and especially good in woodland gardens. Their flowers are borne over a considerable period, but seldom provide much impact. The ordinary form has mauve-blue flowers, whilst 'Alba' has small, waxy, dark green leaves and pure white flowers. The best form is 'Variegata', which has small, leathery leaves of a silvery grey hue which contrasts effectively with its blue flowers. Other forms are 'Rubra', with rosy purple flowers, 'Coerulea Plena', with narrow leaves and double blue flowers, and 'Aureo Variegata', a less vigorous golden-leaved form with white flowers flushed pink. There is also a golden variegated form with blue flowers. With these the recommended spacing is 18 to 24 inches. *Vinca minor* is indigenous to the British Isles, whilst the Larger Periwinkle (*Vinca major*) is generally considered to be a garden escape reputed to have been first introduced from Europe at an early date. It is a much more vigorous grower with arching shoots which will sometimes ramble amongst the lower branches of adjacent bushes without harming them. The larger, light blue flowers are mainly borne on erect new shoots springing from the crown of the plants. The white form which I grow has much smaller flowers. The variety 'Pubescens' is a more erect grower, its bright, violet purple flowers being star-shaped with narrower, twisted petals.

Bergenias, those giant members of the Saxifrage family, whose large, persistent orbicular leaves have given rise to the name 'Elephant's Ears', make first-rate groundcover plants. They produce their large, rounded panicles of pink or white flowers from February to April, coinciding with the main display of camellias. They should be planted in conjunction with rose and pink rather than with red shades of camellia and are particularly effective beneath any of the *C.* x *williamsii* hybrids. The commonest species is *B. cordifolia,* with deep pink flowers, and there are several with rosy-red inflorescences. The hybrid 'Delbees' or 'Balawly Hybrid' combines large glossy leaves with bold rosy-red flower pani-

157

cles, whilst *B. stracheyi* has very large hairy leaves and pale pink or white flowers.

Among dwarf and prostrate shrubs suitable for harmonizing or contrasting with camellias in spring the evergreen azaleas are among the best though only the earliest varieties can be relied upon to flower at the same time. Of these 'Amoena' is rosy purple, 'Hinomayo' is shell-pink, 'Hinodegiri' and 'Christmas Cheer' are crimson, 'Kirin' is silvery pink and there is an early white variety called 'Snow'. Plant these three or four feet apart, or even closer, as they can be transplanted safely later should they become overcrowded. These are often listed in nursery catalogues under *Rhododendron obtusum.*

Among Japanese Quinces (*Chaenomeles,* formerly *Cydonia*) there is one which has a low, prostrate habit. This is the hybrid *'Simonii'* with the darkest of crimson flowers, which contrast best with late white camellias such as 'Mathotiana Alba', 'Haku-Rakuten' and 'Amabilis'.

In milder localities *'Coronilla glauca'* forms a low, rounded bush with small, persistent glaucous leaves and fragrant clusters of yellow pea flowers throughout winter into spring. In wet climates it is wise to remove the tips of the shoots from time to time to maintain a compact shape. The dwarfer *C. valentina* has finer greyer foliage and deeper, more heavily scented flowers but it is very scarce and difficult to propagate.

Among the Cowslip Bushes, *Corylopsis pauciflora* is a real sweetie of unsurpassed daintiness. The slender almost horizontal twigs become smothered with fragrant, pale yellow cowslip-like inflorescences in March and April, a colour which looks particularly well when associated with single camellias with pale yellow stamens such as 'J. C. Williams'.

The early cream Broom, *Cytisus praecox,* with its low, cascading habit, makes an excellent foil for camellias but as it attains a spread of 4 or 5 feet it should not be planted too close to them. A new variety named 'Allgold' contrasts particularly well with *C. japonica* 'Adolph Audusson'. The cream hybrid *C. x kewensis* and *Genista lydia* brooms which are prostrate without becoming invasive.

The winter-flowering heather *Erica carnea* in its many varieties is useful for groundcover plantings, but remember that white forms, such as 'Springwood White', are best planted in association with red camellias. Marriages between varieties of *Erica carnea* and *E. mediterranea* (soon likely to be renamed *E. herbacea* and *E. hibernica* by botanists) have given rise to a number of named hybrids of which the first was *E. x darleyensis,* a more vigorous type with low, spreading habit and bearing a long succession of lilac pink flowers from November to April. Other *darleyensis* hybrids include 'Silberschmelze' ('Norman Webster'), silvery white, 'Arthur Johnson', rosy purple with long, prostrate shoots, 'George Rendall' a compact deep pink and a new seedling which I have christened 'Pink Spangles'. This has the largest and richest coloured bells which eventually turn deep rosy red. The calyx lobes are pale pink and stand out at right angles to the corolla to provide a distinct bicolor effect. It received an Award of Merit from the Royal Horticultural Society in April 1971 as a cultivar of *E. carnea* after several years in the Heather Trials at the R.H.S. Garden at Wisley in Surrey. Plant the *carnea* varieties 12 to 18 inches apart and the *darleyensis* hybrids at 18 to 24 inch centres to provide complete groundcover in two to three seasons.

The bushy lilac-pink Mediterranean Heath (*E. mediterranea*) can be effectively grouped with camellias, the white variety 'W. T. Rackliffe' forming a tight spherical shrublet seldom more than 18 inches in diameter. The Portugese Tree Heath (*E. lusitanica*) is a tall, erect grower which often produces its spires of salmon pink buds followed by white flowers by Christmas, though in some seasons much later. This species grows as tall as most camellias but has a stiffly erect non-spreading habit.

Two species of Genista are suitable for our purpose. The Spanish Gorse (*Genista hispanica*) forms an almost spherical bush about 2 feet high, smothered with yellow flowers in April and May, whilst the already mentioned G. *lydia* is completely prostrate with small golden yellow flowers.

Pieris japonica 'Variegata' is a form of the Lily-of-the Valley bush which remains dwarf enough for foreground planting. The flower buds are coppery pink and remain thus throughout the winter, opening to white panicles in spring. *Pieris formosa forrestii* in its best forms produces young growths so brilliant as to resemble poinsettias. 'Forest Flame' is a cultivar of low compact growth which colours early then fades to creamy yellow with narrow leaves, 'Wakehurst' has broader foliage and comes into growth several weeks later. It has a more open habit and eventually makes a tall, bushy shrub as large as any camellia.

There are many dwarf rhododendrons suitable for inter-planting among camellias. Those which flower early include 'Blue Diamond' (violet blue) 'Blue Tit' (lavender blue) and scintillans (violet purple). *Rhododendron ciliatum* is low-growing with large pale pink flowers in great profusion, whilst *R. williamsianum* is worth growing if only for its low, spreading habit and grey-green orbicular leaves, shaped like those on young plants of *Eucalyptus gunii*. Avoid planting rhododendrons with over-large or brightly colored flowers, as these may well detract from the camellias with which they are associated.

Now let us consider those dwarfer-growing shrubs which provide colour and interest in flower, foliage or fruit when our Camellia master plants have finished flowering.

There are several forms of the reasonably dwarf cut-leaf Japanese Maple (*Acer palmatum* 'Dissectum') of cascading habit which take many years before they exceed three feet in height. The green leaved type is often called 'Viridis' whilst purple-leaved forms include 'Atropurpureum', 'Nigrum' the darkest, and 'Rubrifolium' with reddened foliage.

160

Anthyllis hermanniae, an attractive dwarf shrublet with narrow grey-green leaves covered with small, golden, pea-shaped blossoms in May and June, rarely exceeds 18 inches in height and prefers a sunny situation. It contrasts well with either of the purple-leaved Maples described, as does *Genista hispanica, G. lydia* and the dwarfer shrubbery hypericums mentioned later.

Arundinaria pumila is a miniature bamboo producing dainty, bright green foliage on slender canes a foot or so high. It spreads slowly by suckering but seldom becomes invasive and grows well under trees.

There are several Cotoneasters suitable for associating with camellias. One is *Cotoneaster dammeri* (formerly *C. humifusus*) , a neat evergreen ground-hugger with bright green leaves, white flowers and large red berries often sparsely set. At Caerhays the steep bank facing the forecourt is neatly covered with this useful little plant. A recently raised hybrid between the Willow-leaved Cotoneaster, *C. salicifolius* and *C. dammeri,* aptly christened 'Saldam', is such a vigorous ground-cover plant that its long trailing branches tend to become invasive, but may be used for winter foliage if pruning becomes advisable. *Cotoneaster adpressus,* the Chinese 'Nan-Shan', is also excellent.

Some prostrate Cotoneasters such as *C. conspicuus, C. horizontalis* and *C. microphyllus* have such rigid branches that they might become too dominant if associated with camellias. There are a number of Continental raised hybrids worthy of trial, including 'Skogsholm' and 'Perkeo'.

Incidentally the gender of Cotoneaster was changed from feminine to masculine recently, a favourite trick of researching botanists, who are still at liberty to make such changes without consulting or advising nurserymen of their intentions so that uniform corrections can be made when they revise their catalogues. Consequently it is often the enthusiastic amateur with more time to study horticultural journals who happens across such innovations first, which salient thought brings me to another family of plants containing several suitable for the purpose under discussion—the Hypericums, popularly known as St John's Worts. Harking back to the topic of changes in plant nomenclature, I recall a trip to Holland a few years ago when I visited the Horticultural Proving Station of the highly organized Dutch nursery industry at Boskoop. There some seven hundred nurseries supply a relatively small number of exporters who ship nursery stock to almost every country in the Temperate Zone. I noticed that two Hypericums, both well known in English nurseries and gardens, had been re-named and, within a matter of months, these innovations were copied, as though by a government directive, in every Dutch nursery catalogue.

Enquiries revealed that the research which resulted in these changes had been carried out by the Proving Station. All leading British botanical institutions had been advised, but, as far as I could ascertain, the documents had been either disapproved or filed away unread. So almost overnight *Hypericum elatum* had become *H. persistens* and *H. patulum* 'Hidcote' had become *H. forrestii* 'Hidcote' for reasons concisely stated in the Station's bulletin, and immediately every Dutch nursery followed suit. Perhaps British botanists disagreed.

As a companion to camellias, *H. persistens* 'Elstead' provides attractive candelabra-like clusters of bright salmon-red fruits preceded by small yellow flowers with conspicuous flares of yellow stamens. It closely resembles our native 'Tutsan' (*H. androsaemum*), which has flat clusters of spherical berries, at first bronze-red and later turning black. The latter seeds itself freely in most gardens but seldom becomes truly invasive. Both come into growth late and may be pruned to ground level in winter if desired.

Hypericum calycinum, the Rose of Sharon, is widely used as a ground-cover plant but produces such densely suckering roots that these would probably compete with those of an adjacent camellia. Its hybrid *H.* x *moserianum* is non-suckering and grows into a low, prostrate bush, bearing large yellow flowers with conspicuous bosses of orange stamens in late summer. It is excellent for under-planting among camellias at a 2–3-foot spacing. There are also a number of lesser species which are usually grown as rock plants. Of these *H. olympicum* and its pale form 'Citrinum' are excellent if planted closer at, say, 12–18 inches.

Several of the deciduous honeysuckles may be used to provide spring and summer colour, forming low hummock-like bushes when planted without support. Particularly worth while are the early Dutch Honeysuckle (*Lonicera periclymenum* 'Belgica') , with fragrant pink flowers in April and May, and the Late Dutch Honeysuckle (*L.* p. 'Serotina') , which has more heavily scented flowers of creamy white stained crimson-purple from July to September.

A new cultivar of *L. heckrottii* named 'Goldflame' is also good, with glaucous leaves stained bronze, and plum-purple buds opening to an unusual shade of orange-purple. All of these may be severely winter-pruned if necessary, but the amateur should be warned that such treatment tends to make a plant grow more strongly and not have the effect of reducing its vigour, as may be desirable.

The Korean Bramble (*Rubus tricolor*) possesses all the merits of a good ground-cover plant though it may not be sufficiently hardy in colder areas. It is a lax-growing, spine-free evergreen and is by no means invasive. The dark, polished, heart-shaped leaves are whitened beneath and the stems, which root freely, are clad with soft bristles. It seems to prefer cool, shady conditions and the scarlet fruits have the same sticky feel and piquant flavour as the Japanese Wineberry, which more closely resembles our loganberry in habit.

Ballota pseudodictamus is a relative newcomer to our

gardens. It forms a neat, hummock-like bush, its lax branches being clad with grey, heavily-felted, orbicular leaves. The whorls of small, lilac pink flowers are not very inspiring but the persistent calyces resemble 'Bells of Ireland' (*Molucella*), and the overall sea-green effect of the plant is most pleasing. In common with other shrubs with downy grey leaves it prefers to be planted in an open, sunny situation where it associates well with camellias.

'There are enough prickly people about without introducing prickly plants,' exclaimed an old horticultural acquaintance of mine many years ago. Maybe he had just cause for his remark, but I cannot omit from this chapter *Berberis wilsonae,* a low, prostrate and prickly bush with small, bronzed, orbicular leaves and large clusters of salmon-red spherical berries in early autumn, when the foliage intensifies in colour before being shed for the winter. Its thorns are long and penetrating, so wear thick gloves if you have to weed around it.

Another barberry which is popular for interplanting amongst evergreens is the diminutive, purple-leaved form of *Berberis thunbergii* 'Atropurpurea', called 'Nana' or 'Little Favourite', which grows into a small rounded bush a foot or so tall. The cultivar 'Rosea' has purple leaves with pink variegations on the young shoots.

The Ling Heaths (*Calluna*) may be planted 12–18 inches apart to provide ground cover and late summer to autumn colour. The double-flowered 'H. E. Beale' pearl-pink) , 'Alba Plena' (double-white) , and 'Flore Pleno' (double-lilac) are now being challenged in popularity by even larger flowered varieties such as 'Peter Sparkes' (double lilac-pink) , 'Joan Sparkes' (double mauve) and 'Elsie Purnell' (an improvement on 'H. E. Beale') . Calluna cultivars with coloured foliage require more sun and are less vigorous. These are most colorful in winter and spring.

Other summer-flowering heathers suitable for our purpose include the many excellent named cultivars of the Cornish

Heath (*Erica vagans*) including the· well-known 'Lyonesse' (white), 'Mrs D. F. Maxwell' (salmon-red) and 'St Keverne' (salmon-pink). Although I have made many excursions to the Lizard Peninsula and walked miles across the open moorland I have never found any to match the 'finds' by luckier plantsmen. Newer introductions include 'Diana Hornibrook' (glowing cerise), 'Fiddlestone', a new variety with tapering spikes of deep salmon-pink flowers which emit a faint violet fragrance, and 'Pyrennees Pink', a name reminding one that *Erica vagans* has a Continental station and is not only indigenous to just one area of Cornwall. Plant these 1½ – 2 feet apart as two- to three-year plants and they will soon provide complete ground cover. They look more natural if massed in separate colours rather than mixed.

In open, sunny situations *Caryopteris* x *clandonensis* is an excellent under-plant to associate with camellias. Though leafless in winter, its low spreading branches become clad with grey, lavender-scented leaves and the flat, spiraea-like heads of violet-blue flowers are freely produced from August to October. The named cultivars are generally less vigorous and spreading than the type.

In milder localities two somewhat similar dwarf shrubs with silvery grey, fern-like foliage may be planted to provide foliage contrast. These are *Senecio cineraria* (formerly *Cineraria maritima*) in its several named forms, all with yellow ragwort flowers, and *Centaurea gymnocarpa,* with more deeply divided leaves and clusters of purple thistle flowers. These prefer wind and sun to shade and shelter so that moisture dries rapidly from their foliage.

The scandent Himalayan Plumbago (*Ceratostigma griffithii*) is worthy of trial but tends to flower too late unless in full sun and may be only suitable in milder localities. *Ceratostigma willmottianum* and the dwarf *C. plumbaginoides* are hardier and worthy of trial for their intense blue flowers in late summer and early autumn.

Most shrubby Rock Roses (*Cistus*) are liable to become

165

too tall and vigorous as close companions for camellias. Exceptions are *C. crispus,* a tough, compact bush with crinkled grey leaves and rose-pink flowers from May onwards. *Cistus palhinhaii* is a relatively recent discovery from an isolated location amidst granite boulders on Cape St Vincent. It is a dwarf and compact grower with very dark, gum-coated leaves and pure white, crinkled-petalled flowers in May and June. Although *Cistus purpureus* may reach a height of 5 feet, it grows and spreads with great rapidity bearing extra-large rosy-crimson flowers, blotched maroon at the bases of the petals. This is a real eye-catcher when in flower and has bright evergreen foliage. Keep it several feet away from young camellias as its probable size when planted out of its pot may be deceptive.

Cleyera fortunei (formerly *Eurya latifolia* 'Variegata') is a handsome low-growing evergreen with leaves conspicuously splashed gold and silver with red undertones. It is a distant relative of the camellia rarely producing small single white flowers along the undersides of its horizontal branches.

Coriaria terminalis is a low-growing sub-shrub with frond-like leaves and fleshy-red, fruit-like petals which persist to enclose the fruit. There is a yellow form named 'Xanthocarpa'.

Cornus canadensis is a slow-growing Dogwood of low, suckering habit and bearing large, creamy-white, petal-like bracts surrounding the tiny flowers. It seems to prefer a light, lime-free soil and some shade. It flowers in May and seldom exceeds 6 inches in height.

Danae racemosa (*Ruscus racemosus*) is the Alexandrian Laurel, a dwarf, shade-loving evergreen forming a compact clump of slender, arching shoots bearing well-spaced glossy, bright green leaves, valuable as a cut foliage.

Euonymus fortunei, an evergreen, ground-hugging relative of the Spindleberry, makes an excellent under-cover

166

plant, especially in dense shade. In the form 'Colorata' the leaves turn coppery red in autumn but are not shed as one might anticipate. The variegated form 'Silver Queen' (*radicans* 'Variegata') is much slower with its smaller creamy-white foliage. Several new forms have been raised recently in America.

Fatshedera lizei, an interesting bi-generic hybrid between the False Castor Oil Palm (*Fatsia*) and one of the ivies (*Hedera*), also shows promise as a ground-cover plant for dense shade. The leaves are fairly large with five triangular lobes.

Hedera Colchica 'Dentata Aurea' is the large-leaved Variegated Persian Ivy. The foliage is heart-shaped and conspicuously splashed and mottled cream and gold. As a ground-cover plant it rarely invades nearby shrubs and trees.

The newer cultivar 'Aurea Striata' has a golden mid-leaf variegation.

There are several diminutive Ivies with variegated leaves. I find that the best one for ground-cover is 'Adam' which forms a dense mat of small silvery-white leaves without reversion. A more vigorous cultivar of similar foliage is 'Glacier'. The recently-introduced 'Tres Coupé' is a green mat-forming cultivar with tiny T-shaped leaves curiously arranged in erect, flattened tiers. It spreads slowly and may not exceed 2 feet in ultimate spread, but we have not grown it long enough to know its maximum dimensions. *Hedera helix* 'Goldenheart' (known on the Continent as 'Oro di Bogliasco') is likewise a good ground-cover plant, its golden mid-leaf variegation shows up from a distance but it is somewhat prone to reversion.

In regions of high rainfall and either high enough or close enough to the coast to escape severe spring frosts, there are many dwarf varieties of Hydrangea which will provide an eye-catching display of flowers in late summer and autumn. The red shades, which turn purple in acid soils, are usually

167

the dwarfer and more compact growers. There are now so many named varieties that it would be unwise to recommend any particular ones here. *Kerria japonica* 'Picta', a dwarf, variegated form of the Jew's Mallow, bears dainty leaves variegated silvery white with single yellow flowers along its slender green stems. It is much less vigorous than the commoner green-leaved forms and rarely exceeds 2 feet in height.

Mahonia nervosa is a rare dwarf member of this section of the Berberis family. It bears glossy, pinnate leaves often tinted bronze, on long stiff stalks which make them excellent for floral arrangement. It spreads slowly by suckering and seldom exceeds 2 feet in height. *Mahonia aquifolium* is also suitable.

Mitraria coccinea is the Chilean Mitre Flower. It forms a dainty dwarf bush, occasionally tending to climb, and bearing pendulous scarlet mitre flowers in late summer.

The Japanese Spurge, *Pachysandra terminalis,* is an excellent though slow-growing ground-cover plant. It has dainty, persistent, palmate foliage on short stems and whitish flower spikes in spring. As is usual, the variegated form is slower-growing than the type and has smaller leaves. They should be planted about 18 inches apart. Both are popular in America.

Pernettyas are suitable companions for camellias, providing berries from late summer in colours varying from white to lilac, pink, rose and shades of red to maroon. They may be grouped in separate colours, or together but always include one or two male plants to ensure a good crop of berries.

The Cape Fuchsia, *Phygelius capensis,* is an excellent companion for camellias. It is a more or less evergreen subshrub which spreads by suckering and throws up sturdy, erect shoots to a height of 3 feet, the tops of which are draped throughout summer with pendent tubular flowers, light red on the type, bright red on form 'Coccineus', which also has darker and glossier leaves, whilst the flowers of *P. aequalis* are salmon-pink. All have orange throats.

168

Most of the Shrubby Cinquefoils or *Potentilla* are excellent for associating with camellias. They are dormant and leafless in winter and early spring and many are of low, spreading habit, their growth being recessive and readily swamped by evergreen master plants. The more prostrate ones are *P.* 'Abbotswood', primrose yellow with grey foliage, *P. mandschurica,* a low, hummock-like bush with tiny grey leaves and white flowers, and *prostrata,* which is more spreading than 'Abbotswood' with larger flowers of the same colour. 'Tangerine' is an exciting colour break with flame-coloured buds opening tangerine colour. Unfortunately it fades badly in hot, sunny situations, so it should be planted in partial or complete shade. It is extremely good during periods of prolonged cloudy weather and wet summers; the wet climate of the south-west seems to suit it admirably. It is one of the best for ground cover. All of these should be spaced about 3 feet apart.

Among shrub roses *Rosa nitida* is ideal for our purpose. It is a dwarf, suckering species with single, bright pink flowers and very dainty glossy foliage which turns to brilliant orange and red in autumn. Be sure to buy it on its own roots so that you do not run the risk of introducing briar suckers into your camellia border.

For milder localities there are several prostrate Rosemaries worthy of trial as ground-cover plants. With the exception of the rather tender *Rosmarinus lavandulaceus* from Capri, all are still classified as forms of *R. officinalis* and flower from mid-winter to May according to season and climate. Particularly good is 'Jackman's Prostrate', with light green foliage and china-blue flowers, whilst 'Semiprostratus' forms a vigorous, mounded bush with profusions of grey-blue flowers, larger than on other forms. There are several more, best reserved for coastal gardens. Rosemary is a littoral plant which does not usually take kindly to gardens very far inland.

There are several dwarf and prostrate willows, such as *Salix boydii* which could be associated with camellias but care should be exercised when siting new introductions of unknown vigour. Such a plant is *Salix sachalinensis* 'Sekka', the Fasciated Willow, a vigorous, horizontal branched Japanese cultivar with long, lustrous leaves on mahogany shoots, often producing bizarre, flattened terminal distortions or fasciations which become adorned with catkins before the leaves appear in spring. This plant provides fascinating, long-lasting material for the Ikebana enthusiast.

Several of the shrubby Sages suit our purpose. The red flowering forms of *Salvia neurepia* are both colourful and long-flowering, with pleasantly aromatic foliage. The ornamental forms of the Culinary Sage (*Salvia officinalis*) are dwarfer and more compact; 'Icterina' has leaves variegated green and gold and is lower growing than the type, whilst 'Tricolor', in its best form, has purple leaves variegated pink and red. These make good foreground plants and are best in full sun.

The Cotton Lavenders (*Santolina*) are also useful for interplanting in sunny situations, the fine, silvery grey foliage of *S. chamaecyparissus* acting as a foil for dark, glossy camellia leaves. The form 'Compacta' is less rampant than the type, both producing profusions of golden button flowers held clear of the bush on slender, wiry stems. *Santolina virens* is a green-leaved form with sulphur-yellow flowers. All are aromatic in the manner of chrysanthemums.

A Sweet Box, *Sarcococca hookeriana* 'Digyna', is excellent in the type of woodland shade enjoyed by camellias. It makes a dwarf evergreen shrub of 2 feet or so with glossy, willow-like leaves on purplish stems. In February and March, the leaf axils are clustered with tiny fragrant florets, each composed of four white stamens enclosed with pink bracts. It provides useful cut material and is quite hardy.

There are several dwarf, shrubby spiraeas which are safe to plant among camellias. *Spiraea albiflora* looks like an albino form of *S.* x *bumalda,* having light green leaves and flat heads of pure white flowers in July and August, seldom exceeding 2 feet. *Spiraea* x *bumalda* is best known in its variegated-leaved form, 'Anthony Waterer', with flat, strawberry-red inflorescences. The leaf variegation is spasmodic and only conspicuous on occasional young shoots. Both tend to spread by suckering, which can be encouraged by severe winter pruning.

Two dwarf forms of the Snowberry, (*Symphoricarpus*) with variegated leaves, are sufficiently restricted in vigour for safe planting among camellias to provide dainty foliage effect throughout the summer. *S. orbiculatus* 'Variegatus' forms a low, rounded bush with tiny leaves margined gold whilst 'Argenteo-marginatus' has silvery white margins. Both produce tiny pink berries in autumn.

There are two species of perennial nasturtium which may be safely associated with camellias and be encouraged to ramble over the bushes to clothe them with colour from midsummer to autumn. One of these is the Scottish Flame Flower (*Tropaeolum speciosum*), a somewhat exacting plant in that it demands a cool, lime-free root run. Although it it has roots exactly like bindweed, it is difficult to establish by direct planting and should be purchased from a reputable nursery as a pot-grown plant in May or June, with a foot or more of young growth to prove its viability. This species flourishes in the high rainfall and acid soils of the Scottish Highlands and was originally introduced from Chile. It has small six-lobed leaves and slender twining stems and usually dies down completely in winter. In the R.H.S. Gardens at Wisley it grows over deciduous azaleas on Battleston Hill. It is particularly useful for growing over camellias to provide summer colour and is best established by tipping a six-inch pile of moist granulated peat at the north sides of camellia bushes and planting therein, without disturbing the surface roots of the host plant.

The Peruvian Nasturtium, *Tropaeolum tuberosum,* is as

easy to grow as the former is difficult. It can be planted in any friable soil, either as small, potato-like tubers in spring, or as started plants from pots in early summer. It is much more vigorous than the former species and is densely clad with attractively rounded, five-lobed leaves amidst which the long, arching, crimson flower stalks arise, topped by solitary, orange, larkspur-like flowers with scarlet markings. Apart from producing fresh tubers, which may be harvested without disturbing the main roots of the plant, it is also possible to transplant some of the young shoots soon after growth commences as these usually have fibrous roots below ground. They should be kept shaded and watered for a few days until they become established and will later produce tubers in the normal way. This plant flowers best in a sunny situation.

Several of the dwarfer Hebes or Veronicas are suitable for interplanting among camellias and will provide either summer-flower colour or all-the-year-round foliage effect. Most of the larger-leaved hybrids are too vigorous or only hardy in mild, coastal environments, but those with smaller leaves are usually much hardier. I know from long experience because our nurseries are in such a pronounced frost pocket that most of our Yorkshire customers can grow plants which we have to protect or take under glass in winter. *Veronica armstrongi* has dwarf, spreading, cypress-like growth, coloured old gold, and small white flowers. 'Autumn Glory' is a more erect grower with small, bronze-purple leaves and short violet flower clusters from late summer to autumn.

'Bowles Hybrid' makes a low, spreading bush with tiny leaves and large panicles of pale lavender flowers over a long period. *V. colensoi* 'Glauca' is of dwarf, compact habit with small, waxy, grey leaves and short panicles of white flowers.

Veronica darwiniana is a more vigorous grower with tiny, grey, well-spaced leaves on slender branches and makes an attractive cut foliage. I once isolated a good variegated sport which was not as vigorous as the type. *Veronica diosmaeflora* forms a dense bush with tiny leaves and panicles of fragrant, pale lavender flowers in May and June. *Veronica alpina* is of low, hummock-like growth with very small leaves and white flowers.

Veronica macrantha is the most distinctive, forming a dwarf, slow-growing bush with very large pure white florets an inch or more across, born in small clusters instead of the usual pointed spikes. Two others of dwarf ground-covering habit and small grey leaves are *V. pimelioides* 'Glaucocoerulea' and *V. pinguifolia* 'Pagei', whilst the gem of all the miniatures is *V. teschneri* ('Carl Teschner'). This newcomer forms a completely prostrate bush with tiny green leaves and large panicles of violet-blue speedwell flowers in July and August. Lastly is *Veronica* 'Waikiki', worth growing for its compact mass of small, bronze-purple leaves even if inclined to be shy in producing its intense violet-blue flower spikes.

Viburnum watanabei resembles a miniature edition of *V. tomentosum* 'Mariesii' to the extent that it was first introduced from Japan as *V. tomentosum* 'Nanum Semperflorens'. This dainty deciduous shrub produces a six-month succession of small white lace-cap flowers along slender horizontal branches and its narrow leaves redden as attractively as those of *V. tomentosum* in the autumn. This newcomer to our gardens is reported to have been discovered in Korea.

There is a dwarf Weigela with creamy-white, variegated leaves (probably *W. praecox* 'Variegata') which has profusions of contrasting pink flowers in May and June. More vigorous is the golden-variegated *Weigela florida* 'Nana variegata' with rose pink flowers and foliage retaining its golden leaf margins untarnished into October.

Z brings us to *Zenobia pulverenta,* a dwarf slow-growing shrub allied to *Pieris* and *Vaccineum* and thriving in cool acid soils. The narrow, well-spaced leaves are whitened beneath and the slender branches are draped in June with large, white, aniseed-scented bells, followed by black fruits coated in a white, waxy bloom.

Among herbaceous plants there are several suitable for the

173

purpose under discussion. *Alchemilla mollis* is one which will flourish in sun or shade and produces a low mass of grey-green foilage topped with plumes of sulphur yellow in July and August.

Dimorphotheca barberiae, the only reasonably hardy species, forms large patches of light green foliage, sometimes pleasantly aromatic, at other times pungent. The large starry, narrow-petalled daisies are of a blotting paper pink and born singly on slender stems long enough for use as cut flowers and last over a remarkably long period. It tends to become exhausted after a few seasons and is best split up and replanted every second or third year.

The Plantain Lilies or Hostas (formerly known as Funkias) are excellent for associating with camellias. They come into growth in April and produce large ornamental leaves. Some varieties are covered with a waxy, grey 'bloom' (e.g. *H. matsudana* and *H. fortunei glauca*) whilst others are variegated. *Hosta fortunei* 'Maculata' has the whole mid-leaf suffused gold, the colour tending to fade somewhat later, whilst there are several with white margins such as 'Albo-marginata'.

The 'Wedding Grass' also known as 'Gardeners' Garters' (*Phalaris arundinacea* 'Variegata') produces a mass of broad cream-striped foliage and keeps its colour well throughout the summer. It is very useful for foreground grouping and underplanting.

The 'Ink Plant' or 'Poke Weed' (*Phytolacca decandra*) is both unusual and stately with bold light green foliage and erect pink flower spikes followed by ink black berries. Its overall height is 2 to 3 feet.

There are doubtless many other plants suitable for close association with Camellias, especially trailing and carpeting plants of more diminutive habit. Whatever one plants the object is to restrict future soil disturbance so harmful to the surface roots of Camellias.

174

A camellia suitably underplanted is less likely to be dug around by an absent-minded or ignorant gardener than one surrounded by course weeds or grass.

To summarize these recommendations, and to list further **plants to provide additional colour and interest whilst camellias are in flower:**

Azalea evergreen cultivars
Bergenia
Chaenomeles x 'Simonii'
Coronilla glauca and *C. valentina*
Corylopsis pauciflora
Cytisus praecox and *C.p.* 'Allgold'
Erica carnea and *E. darleyensis* varieties
Erica mediterranea and *E.m.* 'W. T. Rackliffe'
Erica lusitanica
Genista hispanica and *G. lydia*
Lamium galeobdolon 'Variegatum'
Pieris japonica 'Variegata'
Pieris formosa forrestii 'Forest Flame'
Rhododendron dwarf species and hybrids
Vinca minor varieties
Vinca major

Plants to associate with camellias to provide interest at other seasons of the year:

Acer palmatum 'Dissectum' varieties
Anthyllis hermanniae
Arundinaria pumila
Ballota pseudodictamnus
Berberis wilsonae, B. thunbergii 'Atropurpurea Nana' and 'Rosea'
Ceanothus thyrsiflorus 'Prostratus'
Cotoneaster dwarf varieties
Calluna varieties
Caryopteris clandonensis
Centaurea gymnocarpa

Ceratostigmas
Cistus crispus, *C. palhinhaii* and *C. purpureus*
Cleyera fortunei
Coriara terminalis and *C.*var. 'Xanthocarpa'
Cornus canadensis
Danae racemosa
Erica vagans varieties, *Exwilliamsiana*
Euonymus fortunei 'Colorata,' and *E.f.* var. 'Silver Queen'
Fatshedera lizei
Galtheria shallon
Hebe see *Veronica*
Hedera colchica var. 'Dentata Aurea' and 'Aurea Striata'
Hedera helix cultivars
Hydrangea dwarf varieties
Hypericum dwarf varieties
Jasminum nudiflorum
Kerria japonica var. 'Picta'
Lonicera periclymenum 'Belgica; *L. p.* 'Serotina'
Lonicera heckrottii and *L. h.* var. 'Goldflame'
Mahonia nervosa
Mitraria coccinea
Pernettya varieties
Pachysandra terminalis and *P. t.* 'Variegata'
Phygelius varieties
Potentilla dwarf varieties
Rosa nitida
Rosmarinus officinalis prostrate varieties
Rubus tricolor
Salix boydii
Salvia neurepia and *S. officinalis* varieties
Santolina
Sarcococca hookeriana var. 'Digyna'
Senecio cineraria
Spiraea albiflora, *S.* x *bumalba* and *S.* x *bumalba* var. 'Anthony Waterer'

176

Symphoricarpus orbiculatus var. 'Variegatus' and *S.* var. 'Argenteo-marginatus'
Tropaeolum speciosum and *T. tuberosum*
Vaccinium sp.
Veronica dwarf varieties
Viburnum watanabei
Weigela florida var. 'Nana Variegata' and *W. proecox* var. 'Variegata'
Zenobia pulverulenta
Herbaceous plants:
Alchemilla mollis
Dimorphoteca barberiae
Hosta
Phalaris arundinacea var. 'Variegata'
Phytolacca decandra

A SELECTION OF CAMELLIAS FOR SPECIFIC LANDSCAPE PURPOSES.

(a) FOR ACCENT PLANTINGS to flank vistas, garden pathways and steps or to provide vertical contrast amidst low plantings:
   C. japonica 'Adolphe Audusson', 'Mme Le Bois', 'Optima', 'Professor Charles S. Sargent', 'Yours Truly'.
   C x williamsii 'Citation' (believed a reticulata hybrid by the author) 'Donation' 'Margaret Waterhouse', 'Prof. E. G. Waterhouse'.

(b) FOR BANKS camellias of low, prostrate habit:
   C. japonica 'Lady Clare' 'Momijigari' (Higo var.), 'Yuki-Haki', *C. sasanqua* 'Pale Moonlight' and 'Papaver', *C x williamsii* 'J. C. Williams'.

(c) AS INFORMAL HEDGES: *C. japonica* 'Adolphe Audusson', 'Imbricata Rubra' 'Nobilissima', 'Optima'.
   C x williamsii 'John Pickthorn', 'Mary Larcom' and St Ewe'.

(d) AS WALL PLANTS (N. B. Shade from early morning sun advisable especially when siting early flowering varieties. Plant 1 foot clear of face of wall if possible.)
On sunny walls: C. *japonica* 'Donckelarii', 'Elegans', C. *reticulata* 'Captain Rawes', 'Robert Fortune', and Kunming varieties. C. *sasanqua* 'Narumigata', C x *williamsii* 'Caerhays', 'George Blandford', 'Glenn's Orbit', 'St Ewe'.
On shaded walls: C. *japonica* 'Gloire de Nantes', 'Haku Rakuten', 'Nobilissima', C. *sasanqua* varieties 'Crimson King and 'Hiryu'. C x *williamsii* 'Donation', 'Francis Hanger' and 'J. C. Williams'.

XIII

Camellias In Flower Arrangements
Contributed by Bunty Kitson

Flower arrangements add to the joy of camellia growing, for a wise grower can pick to prune and thereby share the beauty of his or her plants with many others, not only in homes and at special occasions, but at flower festivals in cathedrals, churches and village halls, as well as in hotels and office lobbies.

What a pity that no serious attempt has yet been made by modern architects to incorporate illuminated temperature-controlled flower-display cabinets where live flowers can be maintained in an environment protected from modern central heating. Such innovations would make it possible to replace the plethora of plastic flowers which permeates modern society with more inspiring live material.

Flower arrangement is an art which can develop by studying the principles of design, colour and the use of different materials and using them to create an arrangement, combining balance, colour harmony and texture, to produce a purposeful pattern providing transition from pale to dark, from light to heavy, or rough to smooth, in the manner of artists in other spheres.

As a devotee of camellias I list their unique attractions. They have the most elegant foliage which never wilts and they often commence to bloom before Christmas, in the bleakest part of the year, and continue into May and June. Pick them in the coloured bud stage and open them indoors so that they are unblemished by the weather. The single varieties open and last very well when cut, whilst the anemone-and peony-forms have the longest vase life but are best picked when almost fully open. Some of the formal doubles soon lose the centres of their flowers, leaving only the inner petals to form quite attractive poppy-like shapes. This is particularly so with 'Imbricata Rubra'. In my own home they grew up around the bedroom windows to a height of over 30 feet, and it is curious how the earlier flowers faced inwards towards the granite mullions and glass, doubtless because of the warmth radiated from the stonework. It was therefore easiest for me to pick early flowers from the opened windows. I used a special pick-and-hold flower cutter for this purpose as many of them are so difficult to reach.

My 'Tricolor' usually produced some flowers which were entirely rosy-red without any pale flecks, and occasionally I found one or two divided diametrically, one half being rose-red and the other half blush-pink. It was most exciting to use one of these to link the two sides of an arrangement which has all rosy red blooms on one side merging with tricoloured flowers on the other.

From the foot of the plants one could select old, sweeping branches which are ideal for the larger arrangements and for creating the basic principles in Ikebana. Cut camellia foliage will last from six weeks to six months according to temperature and time of year. The leaves are well spaced, elegantly shaped and their glossy texture can be accentuated by wiping over with a light smear of any clear vegetable oil.

When I demonstrate flower arrangements with camellias I like to select a long, sweeping branch, pruned from the interior of an old camellia bush just when the flowers commence to open. Such a branch will provide an extraordinarily long-lasting main placement, firstly whilst in bud, secondly when in flower, thirdly for foliage effect and lastly to reveal its artistic form when leafless. The latter may be augmented with a few short-stemmed camellia blossoms, to form quite large arrangements with a minimum of fresh material, even a year after it has been cut from the bush.

Some varieties produce exciting foliage variegations, sometimes the leaves are half cream and half green, sometimes spotted, sometimes blotched. On my big plants of 'Imbricata Rubra' I occasionally find shoots bearing leaves which are wholly creamy-white contrasting with lime-green terminal buds and nut-brown stems. Without a doubt camellias provide the most interesting foliage of all.

In small, dainty arrangements, as in Dresden china, I like to defoliate camellias and to use the small flowered varieties such as 'Cornish Snow', or its pink counterpart 'Winton', rising out of a groundwork of lime-green hellebores, *Pieris japonica* and Grape Hyacinths in china-blue and white.

I have already mentioned the bold, recurving branches of foliage which can be cut from the bases of old camellia bushes. These are ideal material for creating the flowing lines so essential to form the foundation of a pedestal arrangement. They harmonize well with other such bold material as rhododendrons, magnolias, tulips and long sprays of *Camellia reticulata* var. 'Captain Rawes' or 'Simplex'. The giant white *C. japonica* cultivars 'Gauntlettii' ('Grandiflora Alba') or 'Haku Rakuten' can be used instead of magnolias for the focal point.

Glossy camellia apples, those usually sterile fruits which are produced after a mild spring, add distinction to camellia foliage in late summer and autumn.

An abstract arrangement can best be described as the pattern created between the flowers, stems and leaves. The effect depends on the discriminating selection of material and the careful removal of selected leaves to avoid confusion and overcrowding. As camellias are such important material they are most suitable to use this way and their grey, woody stems create their own design quite naturally.

181

Since traditional Western arrangements have an abundance of flowers, I usually pick some buds just showing colour, some half and some fully open, and, after removing the lower leaves, I skewer-point the ends of the stalks with a sharp knife so that they will be easy to insert into a crowded container, especially where wire netting, pinholders or other supplementary material is used. I then lay them in polythene boxes with a dash of water before fitting their semi-transparent air-tight lids. Sprays which are longer than the boxes can be carefully curled around the inside, and this bending can be used to accentuate their natural curves. In these receptacles they will last well for days and are easy to transport, as the boxes can be stacked one on top of the other. The colour of each variety can be seen through the boxes and they are light to carry.

With my camellias I often use sprays of blue-grey forms of Lawson Cypress with pink flower buds such as 'Triomphe de Boskoop', *Mahonia aquifolium* var. 'Atropurpureum' with purple hellebores and little groups of blue Roman Hyacinths, scillas and other spring flowers. The late creamy-white trumpet Daffodil 'Mount Hood' lasts for longer than other varieties I have tried and I also like to use forced boughs of the double pink Cherry 'Sekiyama' (Hisakura) to give height.

Camellia blossoms, being formal in shape, look well from whatever direction they are viewed. For this reason they are the best of all flowers for table settings, their many exciting forms, colours and petal nuances being sure to provide a talking point. Bear in mind that this type of arrangement should be kept fairly low so that one may appreciate one's guests.

I have invented a novel way of using camellia leaves to hide supporting material, be it wire netting, pin holder or a synthetic compound. I cut some stems immediately above each leaf to give a number of single leaves on short sections of stem. These I call 'push leaves' because I can press them quickly with my thumb into any vacant spaces, taking care to face them so that they continue the natural sequence of those on the nearest branches.

In Japan the different races of camellia are given distinctive treatment in flower arrangements. The Sasanquas signify autumn and are therefore largely stripped of their leaves in order to reveal their branches. *Camellia japonica,* on the other hand, symbolizes spring and is arranged so that the bold, polished leaves act as a foil against which one can appreciate the beauty of the flowers.

I will now describe the manner in which cut camellias were used in ancient times in Japan, an art known to date back some thirteen hundred years. This is the art of *Ikebana,* and camellias were one of the original flowers chosen since they grow wild over a vast area of that country. In old Japan the girls were forced to study this form of flower arrangement in which the use of their native camellias was of major importance. In each house was an alcove or *tokonoma* in which the flowers of the day were arranged by the mistress. They could, of course, be viewed only from the front, but this ancient practice has been discontinued so that modern arrangements show a greater sense of depth and recession from whatever angle they are viewed.

Ikebana stresses the importance of the beauty of the natural lines formed by branch, stem and leaf. The curved line as well as colour harmony and depth are important. The elementary principles involve the careful placing of three branches or flowers. The first and most important, termed *Shin,* represents Heaven, and should have a length not less than one and a half times the sum of the diameter and depth of the container. It should be set ten degrees off vertical.

The second placement, *Soe,* representing Man, is set forty five degrees off vertical and should be three quarters the length of the first branch, *Shin.*

183

The third placement, *Hikae,* representing Earth, should be three quarters the length of *Soe* and set seventy degrees off vertical with an embracing upward sweep. All three principal placements should tend to curve forward and towards each other.

Before final placing, all superfluous shoots and leaves, *Gomi,* should be removed from these three branches in order to create a tranquil pattern. In Japan it is not unusual to leave a pair of scissors beside an *Ikebana* arrangement in case any portion of it offends the eye of a guest.

Jushi is secondary ornamental material, usually flowers, used at the discretion of the arranger.

Tomi is additional foliage, stones, moss or wood necessary to conceal *Kenzan,* the term applied to pinholders. My 'push leaves' are a form of *Tomi.*

The positioning and incline of these basic placements may be reversed or interchanged and one or two may be omitted altogether.

The basic upright style is termed *Risshin Kei,* whilst in the slanting style, *Keishin Kei,* the *Shin* and *Soe* change places.

In Japan these basic styles have to be drawn and practised over and over again before a pupil graduates from bowl arrangements to *Nageire,* tall vase arrangement, and the more advanced creative free-style arrangements, still embodying one or more of these main principles.

The veteran Japanese exponent of *Ikebana,* Choka Adachi, was responsible for organizing the first flower arrangement school in Japan. He claims to have taught as many as one thousand pupils in two days before flying elsewhere to teach a further five hundred each week. His book *Camellia. Its Appreciation and Artistic Arrangement* is my favourite source of information and I am constantly influenced by its infectious pidgin English.

He describes pinholders (*Kenzan*) as 'the thing many nails stand inverted on lead or antimony plate. You can easily

184

fasten cut ends of flowers by inserting them in this fearful little valley of sharp swards' (for swords).

He also advises: 'In a precious glass pot or vase, Kenzan must be put on a gum or vinyl cloth. When you use extraordinary precious vase, cut ends must be wrapped up with cloth or cotton lest they should injure the vase.'

METHODS OF PROLONGING THE LIFE OF CUT CAMELLIA BLOOMS

Hot, dry atmosphere and exposure to direct sunlight, or draught, will shorten the vase life of all cut flowers, which seem to last best in the cool atmosphere and subdued light usually associated with old churches and cathedrals.

Camellia blooms placed in a cool, moisture-saturated atmosphere, such as that obtained in the sealed polythene boxes already described, will often keep fresh for a fortnight when stored in a cool place away from strong light. Storage in the bottom of a domestic refrigerator gives still better results. It is best to keep the stems damp rather than wet, since they last better out of water.

American research has shown that an application of naphthalene acetic acid delays abscission (shedding) of the petals and helps to preserve the blooms. An aqueous solution of 250 parts per million is recommended and can be prepared by simply mixing 50 milligrammes of N.A.A. powder in half a pint of tap water, and larger or smaller quantities *pro rata*. In practice a much lower concentration apparently works. The liquid should be sprayed down into the axils of the petals with a scent spray, giving several squirts from different angles and avoiding contact with the stamens of single and semi-double flowers.

Prior to storage the bases of the stems may be wrapped in cotton wool which has been soaked in the same solution, and any wrapping material, together with the inside of storage

185

containers, sprayed likewise. Napthalene acetic acid can be stored safely for indefinite periods in either powder form or solution without deterioration. Naphthalene acetic acid is often used as a rooting hormone which can be adapted to this purpose if suitably diluted.

This method presents an excellent method of preserving your best blooms for forthcoming shows.

Index

189